# The Challenge
## of the
## Able Child

It is to these children and their teachers that the book is dedicated.

David George
Nene College
Northampton

# The Challenge
# of the
# Able Child

David George

## David Fulton Publishers
### London

David Fulton Publishers Ltd
2 Barbon Close, London WC1N 3JX

First Published in Great Britain by
David Fulton Publishers 1992, Reprinted 1994, 1995

Note: The right of David George to be identified as the author of this work has
been asserted by him in accordance with the Copyright, Designs and Patents Act
1988.

Copyright © David George

*British Library Cataloguing in Publication Data*

A catalogue record for this book is
available from the British Library

ISBN 1-85346-185-7

Typeset by Chapterhouse, Formby L37 3PX
Printed and bound by
The Cromwell Press Limited.
Broughton Gifford, Melksham, Wiltshire

# Contents

# Foreword

There are so many new initiatives in education at the moment that it is extremely difficult for a busy teacher and parent to keep up to date with what is happening. Teachers are supposed to be *au fait* with multi-ethnic education, equal opportunities, information technology, the new National Curriculum and testing, changing examination systems, ever changing course content, the home and environment, and the hidden curricula that children encounter. Here I am suggesting, in addition, that teachers should be very conscious of our more able children and the number that are under-achieving in our schools.

The author maintains gifted and talented children have special needs and special problems, though not all. They also have special, sometimes immense, talent to give to society. We owe it to them to help cultivate their abilities and society to help prepare tomorrow's leaders and talent. More able children are the most precious natural resource in the world and one that cannot be allowed to be squandered. Survival and achievements of the human species owe much to one characteristic – a capacity for creative problem solving. This ability to find new answers to problems remains a vital one. A major objective of more able education is to recognise and foster this special ability. Unfortunately, the pursuit of this, and related objectives, is often plagued with confusion, misconception, doubtful assumptions, exaggerated claims and a lack of communication.

It is every child's right to go as far and as fast as they can along every dimension of the school curriculum without any brakes being put on them. Therefore, every child is entitled to the best programme, the most attentive care, and the greatest love and respect that we can conceive and provide.

With this in mind, it is still reasonable to talk about groups of children who collectively have special needs but are not well served by what is provided, even by what is well provided to typically or average learners. Of course, even the idea of typical average children must be regarded with care. The important question is this: are very bright, more able, gifted, talented – call them what you may, children systematically different from others in any ways that might suggest educational change and adaptations? If we can identify some of these characteristics, then we should be able to justify special recognition and support for these children.

In addition to these goals a denial of the legitimate aspirations of individuals must have special consequences. There is evidence that some of these children who are not recognised and supported become involved in crime and turn to delinquency. The need to nurture the whole child which is emphasised in this book gives a signal that here is an educationally enlightened approach to the question of gifted and able children, in contrast to many of the earlier works which were only concerned with the identification of educational potential as measured by 'convergent' intelligence tests. The approach here is firmly rooted in the multi-dimensional view of intelligence which is more constructive. With this in mind, you have to assist students who are able to take self initiated action and who are capable of intelligent choice, independent learning and problem solving. This would also help to maximise learning and individual development and to minimise boredom, confusion and frustration. It will help them to realise their contributions to themselves and to society as a whole.

Although this book is aimed primarily at teachers, it should be a useful aid for other professionals and parents identifying more able children and becoming more comfortable with them. It also aims to assist the classroom teacher in becoming a more patient and observing teacher, giving them a knowledge base on which to work in defining their objectives and providing for these children; and to raise the awareness of teachers and parents that there are children underachieving in our schools and therefore not reaching their considerable potential.

This book may or may not change the minds of critics who feel that special education for the gifted is unfair, undemocratic or elitist. The list of virtues listed above plus the argument that a true democracy includes a full individual opportunity may not make a dent in their well intentioned defences, but hopefully will go some way to alleviate the myths that have grown up with this movement.

Importantly, the book does not ignore the special identification and programme needs of female gifted students or culturally different, economically disadvantaged, handicapped or underachieving students which many schools do not adequately accommodate, let alone identify the needs and problems of these children. The book falls into two large sections. The first is designed to set the stage for the remainder of the book.

In order to discuss intelligently what should be done for our more able children in the educational system, we must describe firstly who we are talking about, understand the special needs and characteristics of these young people and how to identify them more accurately. The second part of the book looks primarily at the provision for our more able children and strategies for teaching them.

The author would like to express his thanks to numerous colleagues who have supported the writing of this book. To Dr Richard Alexander of School Scene who contributed much of the section on the assessment of intelligence. Caroline Jones for her contribution towards the section on the psychomotor talent area and Sue Leyden for providing details of case studies. Several colleagues have given permission to quote from their writing, including those from schools where the author has worked and where they are now identifying and supporting gifted and talented children. Pauline Vernon not only produced impressive typed work, but also calmly supported the author. Members of NACE, teachers and students contributed in many ways through discussions and anecdotes about these children and their invaluable experiences with them. I continue to learn from them. My apologies to those I have inadvertantly left out or not acknowledged in the text.

In this book it is my hope that all of you who care about gifted individuals will find much that will aid you to discover the excitement, challenge and pleasure of being with these special children as they share the process of growing up.

The waste of human potential is tragic for the community, for the world but especially for the child. The concerto never written, the scientific discovery never made, the political compromise never found – they all carry heavy costs. Thomas Gray notes this loss in his *Elegy Written in a Country Churchyard*

> Full many a flower is born to blush unseen
> And waste its sweetness on the desert air.

# CHAPTER 1

# *What's in a Name?*

> The gifted and talented come in a tremendous variety of shapes and sizes and are clearly not a homogeneous group.　　　　　　　(Harry Passow)

Who are we talking about? Definitions abound and create much confusion. Anyone who takes the trouble to delve into the mass of published material on this subject is likely to be startled, if not confused, by the variety of terms used to describe very able children and the various criteria used to define them. Yet defining 'gifted' and 'talented' is an extremely important matter and surprisingly complicated. Many people still discuss giftedness and talents as if it were a syndrome or a set of recognisable characteristics. It is best seen as an umbrella term for individuals with a wide variety of special abilities. In some areas we do not dare use the words gifted and talented, but we shall do so because we are the only country that does not use these Biblical terms. Indeed, the parable of the talents in the New Testament is a very sad story because the third person buried his talents, so here was our first underachiever! The gifted are certainly not a homogeneous group and the search for general characteristics of giftedenss has not been fruitful, except where a restricted definition has been used. I would suggest that what we should be seeking is to find what represents gifted behaviour in the fields of human endeavour in which we are interested, describe under what conditions such behaviour will emerge and identify ways of developing such behaviour. This will help us get away from pseudo-scientific labelling of children. But for teachers, the term, 'intellectually underserved' has some value. This indicates that the targets of our concern are those who have special learning abilities that have not been matched with an appropriate programme. Thus the identification process involves not just the study of the child's learning characteristics, but also the learning environment.

To some people the concept means the skills of an outstanding athlete, artist or musician, while for others it encompasses the work of a promising mathematician, scientist, writer or poet. Its application to levels of achievement may also differ from above average to outstanding. What is required is a working definition which can serve two purposes: provide an agreed statement to facilitate discussion and enable a positive response to anyone requiring further clarification of their ideas of exceptional ability. A clear working definition must lie between the two extremes being neither too specific – it should not be so narrowly conceived that some children of exceptional ability are excluded, nor too broad and it should not be so indefinite that no clear guidance is given.

The particular definition adopted by a school in its policy for gifted and talented children is vitally important because it will determine who is selected for any special programme. Further, there is a danger that one's definition and consequent identification methods, will discriminate against such special populations as the poor, minority groups, the handicapped, underachieving and even some female students.

Renzulli (1981) noted that a definition of giftedness must:

(1)  be based on research about characteristics of gifted children;
(2)  provide guidance in the identification process;
(3)  give direction and be logically related to programming practices;
(4)  be capable of generating research that would test the validity of the definition.

The terms listed below are just some that the author has encountered: able, more able, exceptional, talented, superior, gifted, higher educational potentials, more receptive learners, more capable learners and higher academic potentials. These terms may or may not refer to the same or similar group of children. There are obvious dangers in making generalisations about any group of people and this is no less true when talking about our very able children.

These observations suggest that although the notion of the gifted and talented child has been generally recognised, the need for a more definitive definition is a new phenomena in our educational systems. But why have the needs for a more exacting definition of the gifted child taken so long to be realised, even when society recognises the general notion of the gifted?

One can respond to the question by citing the following reasons: firstly, identifying the gifted child through performance of the given task was enough. The educational system was felt to be good enough to identify the gifted. That is to say, nobody was interested in establishing the gifted child at the initial stages of the educational system. Secondly, there seems to be a cultural factor in the sense that to be gifted is to be different from the others. The general idea of an individual being different from the others within society cannot be encouraged. Now, having made these observations, it is fair to want to know what has prompted this sudden upsurge to have more precise definitions of the gifted child. Our society has come to realise the importance of having a deep understanding of the gifted child and if possible, to identify the essential characteristics inherent in these so-called gifted children.

This new interest has been influenced by the following factors, among others: firstly, psychologists have become increasingly interested in the functioning of the human mind. In their efforts to understand how the mind works, these professionals have discovered that some individuals in society are endowed with very little potential to be able to perform certain tasks, which most of the average children find rather easy to perform. Psychologists identify these children as those needed to be treated differently from average children. Thus, it was found that, it would be unfair to assess the intellectual performance of intellectually abnormal children even when we realise that the intellectual potential in the two groups is quite different. These facts have resulted in the establishment of special educational institutions, specialist teachers and a great deal of money being put forward to support this work. Those children who are handicapped either emotionally, physically or intellectually, are now supported and this is now a legal requirement. Later it was realised that by dealing with the handicapped children, they were only dealing with one end of the normal distribution curve of children in society. The other end of the spectrum consisted of those children who seemed to be endowed with performance potential that is over and above what the average child in society possesses.

Secondly, education has been realised as one of the inalienable rights for all individuals. This fact prompts governments to make sure that both the normal and abnormal are presented with the most relevant education. This also calls for the most appropriate method of teaching these important but different groups of individuals.

Thirdly, in our modern societies, certain specialised services are identified from time to time. These services may require people with very high intellectual abilities for example. For such cases, society has a duty to identify those individuals who are endowed with particular high abilities to perform specialised services. A case in point is that some countries have now established educational institutions to admit those individuals with high potential in science and mathematics (to help in international competition in space programmes) and sport (international sporting events).

Fourthly the belief that education is one of the inalienable rights of the individuals in our society implies that the cost of running schools is normally very high for any government. It has also been discovered that children with a more than normal potential ability take a shorter time to learn certain tasks than average and handicapped children. If the government is able to identify children with more than potential abilities, it may end up spending less money on them.

Fifthly, some social scientists have discovered that children will engage in anti-social behaviour for lack of anything better to do. These are children who, because of their high potential ability, take a shorter time to accomplish certain tasks, which are difficult for the average child. In a classroom situation, such children may resort to making mischief because they are often idle for some of the time. Thus, it will be important to identify these types of children in order to reduce anti-social behaviour in our school systems and in our society at large.

Sixthly, scholars are interested to understand the nature of a human being, and particularly to establish the limits of their intellectual potential.

Finally, educationalists are agreed that it is every child's right to go as far and as fast along every dimension of the school curriculum in order to reach their considerable potential and this is one of the major aims of education.

Now, if the reasons cited above can stand the test of time, then an attempt should be made to offer an appropriate definition to the gifted child. It is clear that one cannot identify a single purpose as the motivation for wanting to define terms. However, for every definition, some purposes are more pronounced than others. Thus for this book, our main interest is to attempt to reduce the vagueness inherent in the term 'giftedness' as it is commonly used. If we register any measure of success towards this end, then we hope this will be of some use to teachers and parents, as well as social workers, policy makers and the researchers as they deliberate about the gifted and talented individuals in our society.

Discussion on the precise definition of gifted and talented children should begin rather humbly by examining some versions of the term 'gifted' advanced by scholars and other interested groups, led by Plato (the *Republic*). In his attempt to find a lasting solution regarding the best government in his Athenian city-state, Plato indicated that in any community, there are three groups of people: the craftsmen, the civil servants and the philosophers. His classification was based on the potential endowment of the intellectual abilities each class enjoyed. While the craftsmen were endowed with the least intellectual abilities, the philosophers possessed the most. Plato then provided a system of education which would help to sort out who belonged to each group. Thus most people would drop out of the education system while only a small group reached the apex.

This small group consisted of individuals who were the best in handling the dialectics, one of the most abstract and intellectually demanding subjects offered in the Athenian educational system of that day. It was from this small group that the king was to come.

Even if Plato never talked about the gifted as such, it is plausible to infer the notion from the above general observations. If this is granted then one is likely to draw out certain features from the notion of the gifted adopted by Plato. Firstly, the gifted individual exhibits superior intellectual abilities. Secondly, the human abilities considered as gifts are also useful in the service of society in general. Thirdly, only a small percentage of the entire community is endowed with a particular gift. Finally, the potential gift is within an individual from birth, waiting to be developed.

The next definition of the gifted individual to be considered is given by Painter (1980), who states,

> The capabilities which go to make up giftedness are not absolute for all types of societies and stages of economic development. Those qualities which will be considered to represent 'gifts', even if that particular word is not used, will be the abilities which enable individuals to perform those functions which are the most highly prized in their respective communities or who are able to produce the type of artefact in great demand.

The quotation reinforces the observation made about Plato that giftedness refers to some superior abilities which are concerned to be most worthwhile in the eyes of the community that the individual who possesses the gift is a member of. However, while Painter would consider any human ability as a candidate for being a gift, Plato would only consider intellectual abilities. It is also important to note the new feature included within a definition of giftedness by Painter, that human abilities that eventually turn out as gifts depend on both the society and the demands of that particular period.

In another definition by Newland (1976) a gifted or talented child is considered as that one who shows consistent remarkable performance in any endeavour. This definition is consonant with the previous two, regarding as central the place that superior abilities and the worthwhileness enjoyed in the mean of giftedness. But two rather subtle features are floated here; that the superior abilities be demonstrated in the performance of the individual considered as gifted and above that, the superior performance be consistent in the particular individual. This caveat rules out from the definition of the gifted those human superior abilities that are demonstrated only once, or come out by chance. For example, the student who manages to be on top of his or her class in a physics examination by scoring 90 per cent is not to be considered gifted just on the strength of this one particular performance.

Two more definitions of the gifted are in order at this juncture. On the one hand, a gift is said to imply something that is freely given and that as a present, it may be expected to be beneficial to the recipient Painter (1980). On the other hand, giftedness is said to be our own invention rather than something we discover; that it is what society or another wants it to be and hence its conceptualisation can change over time and space, Sternberg and Davidson (1986). We note that the first of the two definitions does add a new feature to the meaning of giftedness, that what is considered a gift should be of some worth from the perspective of the individual involved. However, what might concern any careful observer is the seemingly antagonistic stance that each of the above definitions takes regarding the origin of what is considered as a gift in an individual. Thus, while one of the definitions emphasises the fact that gifts are freely given to an individual and Plato concurs, the other stresses the fact that gifts are among what can be regarded as a human invention. How do we get ourselves out of this difficulty?

It seems to me that rather than the two definitions conflicting over the origin of gifts in an individual, each tends to be underlying an important feature within the definition of human gifts. Thus, one of the definitions has stressed the fact that the human abilities that are considered as gifts have been endowed in individuals freely and naturally. The other definition on the other hand is stressing the fact that the decision as to which human abilities qualify as gifts in an individual fall squarely on the students themselves. In a nutshell, while we are not the author of human potential abilities, whatever human abilities get developed and eventually qualify as human gifts depends strictly on human decisions. These crucial decisions will of course be influenced by what human abilities are in demand in what society and at what particular time. In addition, they are greatly influenced by teachers, parents and the ethos of school.

There is yet another type of definition of the gifted which seems to be rather different from the definitions cited and discussed above. Thus, according to psychologists, the gifted are considered to be those two hundred superior individuals out of one thousand in a given ability; the extremely gifted are those ten superior individuals out of a thousand in a given ability; and the genius as the one top individual out of a thousand in a given ability. This definition emphasises certain features that are also noted in one way or another in definitions cited earlier. For example, one considers that giftedness involves any human ability, be it intellectual, physical or moral and regardless of whether it is useful or not. However, the definition does highlight the fact that a superiority involving a single ability would qualify an individual to be regarded as gifted.

From these definitions cited above, the following features seem to be identified with a concept of a gifted individual so far:

- superior human abilities;
- superior intellectual abilities;
- natural human abilities;
- superior human potential abilities;
- superior human performance;
- consistent human superior performance;
- one whose intelligent quotient is above 100 per cent and among the top two hundred in a homogeneous group of one thousand students.

The greatest challenge now is to find out which of the above features could be considered as legitimate to a definition of a gifted individual and which we cannot accept especially when some contradictions seem emminent.

A quick perusal through the features listed suggests some agreement as to what is central in a definition of a gifted individual. For instance, in all the definitions there seems to be a common agreement that natural superior human abilities are part of the term giftedness. This common agreement is either explicitly or implicitly expressed. The next candidate for consideration is worthwhileness of the human abilities that are regarded as gifts. Here the degree of agreement is high, but not unanimous. However, it seems to me that even those who do not endorse the future worthwhileness as part of the term gifted, are doing so indirectly. This is because, the meaning of worthwhileness is already embedded within the meaning of superiority in the phrase superior human abilities. Thus, if for the moment we take the features discussed here as central to the meaning of gifted, then we can say that a gifted individual is one endowed with superior natural abilities which are regarded as worthwhile. But is this a satisfactory definition of the gifted?

A further critical study of various definitions of the gifted reveals that in every case the gifted individual is always in a minority in a homogeneous group of people. If this observation is correct, then we could improve our earlier definition by saying that a gifted person is that individual within a smaller percentage of a homogeneous group of people who is endowed with one or more superior natural abilities which are regarded as worthwhile. This improved definition seems to take care of all the features that are common in the definition of the gifted individual. However, if it is adopted, many questions have to be raised regarding all the features listed previously.

The way out of this problem is to note that the suggested definition of the gifted provides just the bare minimum; what every definition of the gifted person must incorporate. But beyond that, each particular definition of the gifted must take other factors into account. For instance, those who are interested in the accurate measurement of the superior human abilities are likely to emphasise the performance aspects of the said abilities. On the other hand, educators and others are likely to define an individual as gifted from the perspective of their potential abilities. This is to say that although the two groups acknowledge the central position that superior human abilities occupy in the definition of gifted, each group tends to emphasise a different aspect. Furthermore, there are those, like Plato, who equate superior human abilities with intellectual abilities only.

In the Western world, for example it has been an established tradition to reward intellectual abilities more than any other human abilities. Today, that picture is gradually changing so that for example, superior athletes are being recognised as among the gifted and rewarded accordingly.

As the reader can see, there is no one theory based definition of gifted and talented that is universally accepted and that will fit all programmes as well as all circumstances for our children. The common use of these terms is ambiguous and inconsistent, for example, it is common and acceptable at the moment to use the terms interchangeably as when we describe the same person as being a gifted musician or a talented musician.

Two well known researchers in this field, Renzulli (1984, 1986, 1987) and

Treffinger (1986) prefer the phrase 'gifted behaviour' which can be developed in certain students under certain circumstances.

Ogilvie (1973) prefers a broad definition which is sufficiently flexible and inclusive. He suggests that to be gifted is to be outstanding in general or specific abilities in a relatively broad or narrow field of endeavour. In this broad definition, he suggests that six areas could be considered: physical talent; mechanical ingenuity; visual and performing abilities; outstanding leadership and social awareness; creativity; and high intelligence. Ogilvie goes further, and from his research states that 3 per cent of our children in England are broadly gifted across the curriculum, but 36 per cent have individual talents, and this may be one way out of our dilemma of finding the right definition. Gagne (1985) concludes that gifts versus talent should reflect the psychological distinction between ability versus performance. That is, the gifted person is one who is distinctly above average in intellectual, creative and other general ability domains, where talent refers to distinctly above average performance in fields of certain activities, such as mathematics, music and art. Ogilvie's definition is also very similar to the US Office of Education's (1972) definition with its multi-talent approach and is one of the most commonly used definitions in the world, which states

> gifted and talented children are those identified by professionally qualified persons who, by virtue of outstanding abilities, are capable of high performance. These are children who require differentiated educational programmes and services beyond those normally provided by the regular school programme in order to realise their contribution to self and society.

It states further that children capable of high performance include those with demonstrated achievement and/or potential in any of the following areas: general intellectual ability; specific academic aptitude; creative or productive thinking; leadership ability; visual and performing arts; and psychomotor ability. This definition has such an appeal because it recognises not only high general intelligence, but gifts in specific academic areas as well as in the arts, and such human attributes as creativity, leadership and psychomotor abilities. It further recognises that gifted and talented students require differentiated educational programmes beyond those normally provided for the majority of our children. It also recognises the two basic aims of gifted children programmes which are to help individual gifted and talented children to develop their potential and to provide society with educated people who are creative leaders and problem solvers. It is also to be noted that demonstrated achievement and/or potential ability takes into consideration the underachieving students who may not be demonstrating their gifts and talents in our schools.

Later in 1978, the US Congress revised Marland's definition that psychomotor ability was excluded because it concluded that artistic psychomotor talents such as dance could be included under the performing arts and that talented students in sport are well provided for in our schools.

This is probably true in the Western world and increasingly elsewhere, because identifying able children in sport is prestigious for both school and country, and on the whole, these children are well provided for with extra coaching, equipment and a great deal of competition. In addition, they are encouraged and rewarded for their efforts. However, Treffinger and Renzulli (1986) said of this definition that the categories are frequently ambiguous, undefinable, overlapping and are frequently adopted with no regard for their actual implications for identification or classroom teaching.

As increasingly educators believe that descriptions of gifted persons are those who make valuable contributions to society, then Renzulli's (1986) argument that gifted behaviour reflects an interaction between three basic components of human ability and these being above average in general or specific abilities, high levels of task commitment (motivation) and high levels of creativity. He believed that gifted and talented children are those possessing, or are capable of developing these traits and who apply them to any potentially valuable area of human performance. This results in gifted behaviour. Taylor's (1978) multi-talent totem pole model raises our awareness that most students possess special skills and talents in some variety. There is a serious problem here however, in assuming that all children are gifted. However, his broad definition of giftedness may be best viewed as an appropriate way to understand, perceive and teach all our children and this book is about good practice in schools.

As a consequence of this discussion, it appears that vagueness is a logical necessity within the definition of a gifted or talented person. Thus, it is not possible to eliminate vagueness from the definition of a gifted person. The best we can do is to clearly understand it and act accordingly for the benefit of our children. There is obviously no one final and agreed definition of gifted and talented. The specific definition that any of our programmes for these children accepts, will determine the selection instruments and procedures, and from our programmes comes a definition of who is gifted and talented, that is, who receives a special training and who does not.

As with so many definitions of exceptional students these are somewhat subjective. There is still considerable debate as to what constitutes outstanding abilities or high performance capability. One could argue that almost all children are gifted or talented in some way. It is just a matter of finding the individual person's talent. Taylor (1978) maintained that virtually everyone has special strengths and theoretically, therefore, could be considered gifted or talented.

Lloyd Spencer of Moi University, Kenya, at the first East African Conference on gifted education in 1991 said, 'one definition of a gifted child is a child who makes definitions of giftedness irrelevant'.

As there are currently 213 different definitions of 'giftedness' and a proliferation of terms such as gifted, talented, more able, exceptional, marked aptitude, then teachers should devise their own working definition. All definitions are by nature generalisations, as all pupils are different. A near definition based on the possession of a high score of general ability, say an IQ of 140, is neither proof nor credible as we approach the year 2000.

The Marland (1972) and Ogilvie (1973) definitions are similar and the best, but in Britain, which now has a National Curriculum, then the following is worth serious consideration in the future.

Gifted and talented children are those who are functioning at the upper end of that particular key stage or one key stage ahead and whose abilities are so well developed and so far advanced of their peer group that a school has to provide additional learning experiences which develop, enhance and extend the identified abilities. The debate continues and the jury is still out!

Before concluding this chapter there is a special category of importance that the reader should be aware of and this is the particular problem of the underachieving child. This is not new as witnessed by the following examples.

**Lessons from childhood**

Creative and imaginative people are often not recognised by their contemporaries. In fact often they are not recognised by their teachers either. History is full of examples.

*Noel Coward* 'When Noel was still two the doctor pronounced that his brain was much in advance of his body and advised that he should be left very quiet, that all his curls should be cut off and that he was to go to no parties'

*David Bellamy* School report – 'Bellamy is a good fellow, is maturing well but is academically useless'

*Roald Dahl* English report at 16 – 'The boy is an indolent and illiterate member of the class'

*Albert Einstein* School report – 'mentally slow, unsociable and adrift forever in his foolish dreams'
Einstein, that gifted synthesiser of the time–space continuum, was four years old before he could speak and seven before he could read.

*Ted Allbeury* He left school to go into a foundry and was told he was 'on the dust-heap of life'. He started writing at 55 after a major upset in his personal life.

*Scott Hamilton* His growth was stunted at a very early age and he was a very sickly child. It was suggested he tried activities such as ice-skating. He became World Champion on four occasions.

*Dame Alicia Markova* She was taken to the doctor because she had flat feet. He suggested ballet!

*Stephen Wiltshire* 'A foolish wise one' (IQ 60). 'I have never seen in all my competition drawing such a talent that this child seem to have . . . Stephen is possibly the best child artist in Britain' (Sir Hugh Casson).

*Isaac Newton* One of our greatest scientists did poorly in high school.

*Beethoven's* Music teacher once said of him 'As a composer, he is hopeless'
*Abraham Lincoln* Entered the Black Hawk War as a captain and came out
  as a private.
*Winston Churchill* Failed examinations

These people were probably identified as underachievers in school or
misfits.

## Underachievement

In this movement we now refer to gifted and talented and underachieving
children. The phenomenon of underachieving is both a challenging and
puzzling one. Puzzling in its complexities and challenging in the significance
of the reversal of this costly syndrome. Space will not permit much
discussion of this important subject, but the reader is referred to the
excellent books by Nava Butler-Por (1987) and Sylvia Rimm (1989).

Gifted children are at high psychological risk in that their unique
intellectual and creative abilities make them vulnerable at home and school
pressures which may initiate underachievement. Underachievement is a
discrepancy between a child's school performance and some index of his or
her actual ability, or the performance in scholastic attainment which is
substantially below predicted levels. Gardner (1961) states 'the fact that a
large number of American boys and girls failed to attain their full
development must weigh heavily on our national conscience'. In England,
numerous HMI reports give evidence from school surveys of many of our young
people underachieving and not reaching their considerable potential. The
above definitions are based on test results, which generally have their
pitfalls and in the case of the dynamic nature of underachievement are
particularly problematic. Since many schools do not habitually administer
intelligence and achievement tests, teachers should employ alternative
methods of identification, which employ the resources available to them
within the normal classroom situation. This information can be gleaned
from various sources ranging from understanding the behaviour and
recognising the characteristics of underachievers to diagnostic teaching
methods and collecting relevant data, such as that which can be gleaned
from children's records, and consulting parents as well as enlisting professional help.

Studies of gifted underachievers have identified characteristics that are
typical of these children. These can be categorised into three levels in terms
of their causes and symptoms. The most important characteristic, which
appears to be at the root of most underachievement problems, is low self
esteem and this seems to lead to the secondary characteristic of academic
avoidance behaviour. This in turn leads to poor study habits, unmastered
skills, poor peer acceptance and lack of concentration in school.

Teachers and parents are advised to observe children over several weeks to determine if a child possesses any of the following characteristics. If a child exhibits ten or more of these listed traits it is recommended that an individual intelligence test should be administered to establish whether the child is gifted but underachieving.

*Profile of an underachiever*

- poor test performance;
- orally knowledgeable but poor in written work;
- superior comprehension and retention of concepts when interested;
- apparently bored;
- achieving below expectations in basic subjects;
- restless or inattentive;
- daily work often incomplete or poorly done;
- dislikes practice work;
- absorbed in a private world;
- tactless and impatient of slower minds;
- prefers friendship with older pupils or adults;
- excessively self-critical;
- unable to make good relationships with peer group and teachers;
- emotionally unstable – low self esteem, withdrawn and sometimes aggressive;
- has wide range of interests and possibly an area of real expertise.

Parenting of the gifted child will be discussed later in this book, but at this point research shows worse male achievement for boys in father absent homes and worse maths and problem solving skills for both sexes in such homes. Successful career mothers serve as effective models for achieving girls. Parents have a crucial role to play in identifying these children, but above all in supporting them at home and encouraging them in development of academic, artistic and sporting skills to name but three. At the same time, it is important for children to receive the right balance between encouragement and correction. Children should be helped to avoid manipulating their environments instead of making real effort.

These and the following characteristics encourage underachievement in our children:

- inflexibility and rigidity in schools;
- stress on external evaluation;
- a perceived lack of genuine respect from parents or teachers for each individual child;
- a competitive social climate;
- dominance of criticism from both home and school;
- an unrewarding curriculum;
- a lack of opportunity to communicate what they have learnt; and
- work too easy or tasks lacking in purpose.

As we have briefly discussed the underachieving gifted child continues to underachieve because either the home, school or peer group support that underachievement. The child is possibly not motivated to achieve and there are probably deficiencies in skills necessary for achievement. Thus the child working below his or her ability affects both their educational success and eventual career achievement.

The cure for underachievement is best summed up in Rimm's model (1989), she has found that the treatment of underachievement involves the collaboration of school and family in the implementation of her model:

- The first step in the underachievement reversal process is an assessment that involves the co-operation of the educational psychologist, teachers and parents.
- Communication between parents and teachers is an important component of the cure for underachievers. This should include a discussion of assessed abilities and achievements, as well as formal and informal evaluations of the child's expression of dependence or dominance, and these are particularly important in order to avoid reinforcing these problem patterns. This may again involve an educational psychologist and at least a wise school counsellor or tutor group leader.
- Changing expectations are often difficult because sometimes both parents and teachers have low expectations of children, due to various factors, but it is important to underachieving children that parents and teachers are able to honestly say to them that they believe in their ability to achieve higher. Bloom's (1985) studies of talent development found that parents of research neurologists and mathematicians always expected their children to be very good students. In contrast the author undertook some work in a very poor part of Liverpool in a solid, but dilapidated late Victorian school, overlooking the Mersey flanked by council houses and back to back terraces. Pupils from this school came from the immediate locality with its poor housing, high crime rate and chronic unemployment. A quarter of the children belong to ethnic minorities. The overall problem is low aspirations of many of the pupils and low expectations from parents. Evidence for this is that less than 4 per cent of pupils get four or more A to C Grade, GCSE's and only one in four stays into the sixth form. Eleven percentage points less than the national average.
- Sir Christopher Ball, who is leading a study for the Royal Society of Arts into why so many young people drop out of education at 16, says 'there is nothing wrong with the English system of education and we must guard against the idea that young people are either stupid or sunk in low aspirations'. Young people in areas described above get their negative attitude to education from their parents – working class dropouts beget working class dropouts and even more intensively from

their peers. However, in the school described there are still steps being made and excellent staff doing their best to improve this school environment that expects and values high achievement.

- A critical turning point for the underachieving child is the discovering of a model for identification. As noted above, Bloom's biographical research with highly intelligent students shows that parents model the values and life styles of successful achievers in the talent area. When a parent is perceived as competent and strong, pleased with their job and permits their children to master tasks independently then this makes for an ideal family environment for a gifted child. Since this ideal family situation is rarely provided for the gifted underachiever then parents and teachers need to help the student find a good model for identification and this often is the class, or subject teacher, or a good outside mentor, who has been matched to the individual child very carefully.

- The behaviour discussed in step one will identify some of the areas where reinforcement at home and school will help the underachieving child. These may take the form of rewards which are meaningful to the child and should be within the value system of parents and child, as well as being within the capabilities of teachers to administrate.

Above all these children need, from both parents and teachers, patience, dedication and warm, encouraging support.

Butler-Por (1987) concludes that we should adopt a multi-dimensional approach to the problems of underachieving children, providing an appropriate educational environment in the classroom and utilising teaching methods capable of answering children's needs, which can contribute towards reversing underachievement in young children of all ability levels.

Since teachers often encounter difficulties in recognising both the diversity of potential and the specific needs of underachievers in their classes, this book encourages both them and the parents of the children in their charge to better understand the capabilities, needs and behaviour of children, so that they can initiate the appropriate intervention and plan the kind of educational environment and learning experiences capable of breaking the cycle of failure in some children.

As we learn more about the characteristics of gifted and talented children, we find that many of them have been overlooked, for example, handicapped students, students from minority backgrounds and even some girls. Harvey and Steeley (1984) administered a battery of tests at a correctional centre and found 18 per cent were gifted. They also noted that the pattern of their abilities were not consistent with classroom related tasks. Clearly the need to identify special groups of giftedness in students is one of the greatest challenges facing those of us interested in this field. Culturally different children are also difficult to identify. Coleman (1985) noted that the number of gifted students from non-white, non-middle class, non-urban backgrounds is disproportionally low. Identification amongst these types of students is difficult, because they typically score lower than average on traditional tests of intelligence and achievement. It is difficult to find research to indicate why this is. Some say that the tests themselves are biased whereas others support the idea that these children score low because of the lack of opportunity to develop and grow intellectually. Here is a challenge for further research, but it is apparent that these students from minority groups, or impoverished backgrounds, have the potential if given the opportunity to achieve highly.

The education of gifted girls has historically been largely ignored. In the workforce, women continue to be under-represented in the most traditional male professions and salaries are comparatively poor. No country in the world can afford to lose 50 per cent of its national potential. Although in many countries gifts and talents of girls are being recognised, there is still a long way to go. Historically the main problem is the home–career conflict and although there is no easy solution some women decide in advance to compromise the career to fit husband and family needs.

Peer attitudes and expectations often depress female achievement and school expectations reward male independence, confidence and aggressiveness, but reward female conformity. There is some evidence to suggest that some all girl classes and all girl schools may help some girls take leadership positions, as well as courses they might otherwise avoid, such as mathematics and science.

This special problem that characterises the wide reaching cultural underachievement of women requires that all persons be enlisted in the tasks of changing the culture, in order to support the development of women. The rewards to individual girls and to our society as a whole will make the effort most worthwhile.

# CHAPTER 2

# Characteristics of Gifted and Talented Children

> Children never give a wrong answer...they merely answer a different question. It is our job to find out which one they answered correctly and honour what they know.
>
> (Bob Samples)

Having discussed at some length a definition of the children we are here considering, it is suggested that we use as a working definition for the remainder of this book the following: gifted students are those with a potential to exhibit superior performance across a wide range of areas of endeavour. Talented students are those with a potential to exhibit superior performance in one area of endeavour.

It is important to realise that gifted and talented students are not a homogeneous group. They do not exhibit the same traits or characteristics, but rather a wide range of individual differences. No single trait itself constitutes giftedness. Gifted and talented students often exhibit superior abilities and task commitment, not necessarily in pro-social ways or within the school curriculum. Both gifted and talented students are frequently creative.

Children's gifts and talents may become apparent at different stages of their lives. A child may exhibit talents in one area, for example art or music, or in a combination of areas. Gifted and talented children are present in all groups in society, including those requiring remediation in certain subject areas.

This working definition of gifted and talented students indicates that they can possess superior capabilities in a number of areas. Those areas are recognised as being intellectual, academic, creative, social or leadership, as well as psychomotor. It is also important to recognise which characteristics these children do not have. Not only does the general public have misconceptions about these children, but also many educators do. There has been much misinformation about characteristics of these individuals, and particularly about personality characteristics. Many people assume that these children are in some way different. Case studies of these individuals frequently include the adjectives neurotic, socially inept and lonely. Research, however, has repudiated these descriptions. Most of the myths are based on stereotypes of gifted students as a group. Obviously each student who is gifted or talented will have different strengths, personalities and characteristics, just like all children have. For example, Lock and Jay (1987) noted that gifted girls reported a more positive self-concept than did their non-gifted peers, whereas gifted boys reported a lower self-concept than did their peers.

Lewis Terman who was actively involved in the development of the Stanford-Binnet Intelligence Scale followed 1,500 gifted individuals over 30 years, and some of that work still continues today. This has been the most significant research about gifted individuals, and all these people had IQs over 140, which is a very high cut-off point. Data collected indicated that this group were well adjusted, had superior physical characteristics and made a successful transition into the working world, frequently becoming leaders in their professions.

The data also indicated that these children were advanced in reading, language usage, arithmetic reasoning, science, literature and the arts. The data collected, however, indicated that the gifted children's superiority was less marked in certain areas such as spelling and history Terman and Oden (1959). It was also apparent that not all these children had the same strengths and weaknesses. More recently, Freeman (1991) traced 169 young people from a previously detailed study of 210 5–15 year olds. These studies have done more than most to take the myths and stereotypes out of the contentious and emotive subject of gifted children and their education. The recent research is a fascinating picture of how different kinds of homes and schools deal with intellectually outstanding children, and how the children themselves react both to their unusual abilities and to their education. Many of these children are now at university, but others have dropped out after choosing unsuitable courses, or, in the case of working class students, facing astonishing class snobbery at the prestige universities. Others were unemployed, and some had suffered from considerable depression and loneliness. Many had received virtually no advice about educational choices and careers, even though they were good at almost everything, though choices were difficult. One of the problems identified was that the children were only really offered one target, and that was to go to university, and that schools tried to eke out every ounce of academic achievement, whereas they needed a wide range of opportunities outside the academic curriculum, as they had potential for many things. This stressful situation is not really as awful as might at first be perceived. George (1990) sees a superior sense of humour in most gifted children following quite naturally from their ability to think quickly and see relationships and this is confirmed by Clark (1988) and others. Their humour often appears in art, creative writing, social interaction, and is a part of their general confidence. In addition, when considering a definition of gifted individuals, creativity always enters into the picture. Many discoveries, inventions and artistic creations are the result of 'fooling around' with ideas and playing with possibilities.

## Characteristics of the creative child

An area in which gifted and talented children often excell is creativity, though the intellectually gifted child may not be creatively gifted as well. The brighter children tend to do more creative work and score high on creativity tests. However, after an IQ of about 100, the relationship drops to virtually nothing. This means creative and intelligent characteristics of these children might be quite independent of each other. Fortunately, creativity is an extremely difficult concept to define and subsequently to measure. It is certainly something to do with our perception, intuition, consciousness, thinking skills and problem solving, as well as the use of our senses. The term, in fact, has multiple meanings and can be defined quite differently by a variety of people (Klein, 1982).

It is most important to distinguish between intelligence and creativity when we select students for special programmes in our schools. It is all too easy for teachers to select those who conform, are prompt, neat and 'teacher pleasers', rather than those creative children who are less conforming. Some of the earlier and most interesting work in this area was conducted by Paul Torrance (1977), who devised tests of creative thinking which will be discussed in Chapter 3. Torrance produced a check list for creative students which makes the creative person look really good. Characteristics include: skills in group activities, problem solving, the ability to express their emotions easily, keen sense of humour, originality and persistance in problem solving. They are curious, have high energy, are idealistic, have artistic interests and are keenly attracted to the unusual, the complex and the mysterious.

Torrance (1981) gave an additional list of common characteristics of the creative child which may be helpful to parents and teachers in recognising these children. The list includes:

(1)    is full of ideas and sees the relationship between them;
(2)    is imaginative and enjoys pretending;
(3)    has flexibility of ideas and thoughts;
(4)    constructs, builds and then re-builds;
(5)    can cope with several ideas at once;
(6)    always telling others about their discoveries or inventions;
(7)    likes to do things differently from the norm.

However, Torrance also gives a list of characteristics which may be negative and, therefore, irritate parents and teachers. These include:

(1)  stubbornness;
(2)  unco-operativeness;
(3)  non-participation in certain activities;
(4)  low interest in details and indifferent to some common conventions and courtesies;
(5)  disorganised and sloppy about matters which appear unimportant;
(6)  temperamental, demanding and emotional.

Both these lists indicate the diversity of creative abilities, as well as the difficulty of relying on a check list only (see Chapter 3).

Because of the numerous areas in which a student can be gifted and talented, it is not surprising that there are probably as many different strategies and policies for identifying these children as there are definitions. If we have accepted that gifted children should be those who are defined as children who consistently excel or show the potential to consistently excel above the average in one or more of the following areas of human endeavour to the extent that they need and can benefit from specially planned educational services beyond those normally provided by the standard school programme. A broad definition should consider the following talent areas.

(1)  General intellectual ability
(2)  Specific academic aptitude (an aptitude in a specific subject area)
(3)  Creative and productive thinking (divergent thinking that results in unconventional responses to conventional tasks)
(4)  Leadership and social awareness ability (assumes leadership roles, but also is accepted by others as a leader)
(5)  Visual and performing arts ability (graphic arts, sculpture, music or dance)
(6)  Pyschomotor ability (mechanical skills or athletic ability)

But each child is unique and all attempts at defining these children is a generalisation. It is impossible to cover every individual variation of ability and talent which is what makes this work so fascinating. However, defining gifts and talents is important because the particular definition and recognisation will determine the selection of children for special provision. The poor, ethnic minority groups, handicapped, underachieving and female gifted children may be discriminated against.

## Case studies of four very different children

Case studies of gifted and talented children can help us recognise many of the characteristics of these children and identify their needs. After each subject summary, there are questions for discussion and some suggestions for helping the child. These cases are recommended for in-service workshops or simply to help readers focus in on these children.

The first three case studies may give the false impression that all gifted children have problems. Hitchfield's (1973) and Freeman's (1991) research gave us no evidence to suggest that there were more problems amongst these children than any other group. Most gifted children do consistently well and are happy well-balanced people. Some schools have their ample share of gifted children with 98 per cent taking A levels and going into higher education, and few of them have problems.

Francis is one case of a positive success where both parents and school cope well to make an able child happy and high achieving in most areas of the curriculum.

### Paul, aged 5½

*Background information*

David is the second of two children. The older child Sarah, aged 7, is a quiet little girl, doing well in school, but not outstandingly undemanding and rather undemonstrative at home. David, by contrast is very prominent. At home he takes up a great deal of his parent's time and energy. He is boundlessly energetic, sleeps only six hours a night, exhaustingly interested in everything around him, spends hours dismantling everything mechanical or electrical. He had to be withdrawn from playgroup because staff were unable to manage his behaviour with other children. He has few friends in the neighbourhood and his parents feel 'criticised' about their management of their child.

He was admitted to school early at his parents request. He already reads fluently, with the accuracy and understanding of a much older child. However he dislikes the process of writing, declaring it to be 'boring', and will only do so under duress. His ability to work with numbers is quite advanced. He can add and subtract with numbers up to 100, and enjoys working on number problems in his head. He has periods when he will concentrate intensely, almost obsessively, on a task which captures his interest, but for the most part he moves about restlessly, visiting other groups to see what they are doing, making comments and suggestions to them (usually resented), or actively interfering or disrupting their play. He has become unpopular both with children and staff, and is becoming quite a problem. Paul shows considerable ability in that he learnt to read early, has good number skills and high level of conversation. However, his behaviour is destructive and he is rejected by other children.

*Points for discussion*

School
(1)  What would you see as being David's educational and social needs?
(2)  How might these be met within the school?

Parent
(1) What would you see as being David's needs – from school?
(2) What does David need from you and the family?
(3) How might you assist the school?
(4) What other forms of support would you welcome?

*Some suggestions to help Paul*

Maybe he is in the wrong school as they are not catering for a bright boy. He needs a very skilful teacher who could harness his energies and interference with other children and get them on his side.

*Educational needs*

- Discovering an interest in writing/presentation (using a computer, tape recorder, visual materials, word processor), he must find it worthwhile getting his work on view.
- Learning to stick with a task. Setting criteria for completing something and insisting it gets done to that criteria. If he were older he could be given a contract (see p. 90).
- Accepting time limits for teacher attention and non-interference of others. Use of a clock which he can watch to see when he can change tasks and visit other areas, can be motivating.
- Being given interesting and stimulating problems to solve, such as in maths which tax his ingenuity, instead of routine computations.
- Constructive use of his reading abilities – opportunities to do something for others with these abilities.

*Social needs*

- Accepting class rules and expectations.
- Learning to take part in group activities.
- Coping with frustration (teacher patience with acknowledgement to Paul that they understand why he's angry).
- Plenty of variety in activities, with gradual extension of the time he spends on them. Some physical activities before bed may help him sleep!
- Tolerance from teachers.
- Sense of humour from teachers.
- Sharing with other teachers – ideas, help, sharing of time, Paul could spend some time with others, or with head teacher.
- Finding what he likes to do most and using this as a reward.
- Advice and support from parents. It would be interesting to check Paul's diet as some foods which contain additives can cause hyper-activity.

- Advice and support, and programme planning from the school educational psychologist.
- Suitable materials to meet his interests in things mechanical and dismantling.
- Six hours sleep is no problem – give him access to a light, his toys and books and explain to him what the needs of others are – more sleep, private time, etc.

### Elizabeth, aged 10 +

*Background information*

Elizabeth is an only child. Her parents were in their late thirties when she was born. Elizabeth was precocious as an infant, learning to read when she was two, and showing an unusual talent in a number of fields. By the age of five she was reading books usually thought suitable for twelve year olds, she started learning the piano and the guitar, and was taking dancing lessons. At twelve she is still an excellent all-round achiever, playing the piano, the clarinet and the guitar, she is a member of the local gymnastics team and produces a consistently high level of work in school.

However, in school Elizabeth is not terribly popular. Her achievements and abilities are recognised but no-one feels very comfortable with her, she is rather tense and brittle as a person, and tends to make teachers and pupils feel rather second-rate and inadequate. She does not suffer fools gladly and is quick to put people right. Although she produces high quality work she reacts very badly to any adverse comments, and shows great distress when anything but praise is given to her work. Nothing less that consistent A grades satisfy her.

Elizabeth's parents do not mix easily and they appear a very self-contained couple. They are enormously proud of their daughter's success, and devote much, if not most of their time, to supporting her in her activities.

Despite her apparent successes Elizabeth does not seem to be enjoying her life as much as she might. She appears to have been mismanaged at school with no negotiation of her role, and low self esteem.

*Points for discussion*

School
(1) What do you see as the major concerns in working with Elizabeth?
(2) What do you think needs to be done to help Elizabeth continue to achieve at an appropriate level for her abilities, but which would help her out of the stress of striving all the time for top grades?
(3) What could teachers do to help Elizabeth feel more at ease in her

relationships, and less destructively demanding of herself and others?
(4)   What are the danger areas in the future for this child?
(5)   What would you want to be talking about with her parents? What help might you want from them?
(6)   How might you work with the parents?

*Some suggestions to help Elizabeth*

I would suggest that Elizabeth has been mismanaged at school as there has been no negotiation of her role.

(1)   Her manner tends to antagonise, therefore teachers may want to 'put her down'. Positively encouraging her academic achievements may increase her arrogant behaviour and further distance her from her peers socially. Introducing safe areas for her to meet with difficulties is vital. The question will be how can this be done without producing the negative response she tends to show? – finding ways in which she can work co-operatively with others. A change of school is a last resort where she could be counselled and given a fresh start.
(2)   She must be set tasks for which there are no assessment outcomes.
(3)   She must be set tasks which call for the collaboration and co-operation of others. Joining in team games and the school orchestra would be helpful.
      She must have open-ended tasks and problems which offer a range of different routes, outcomes. She must be faced with tasks *beyond* her present capacity with a planned strategy for helping her face her feelings when she is not able to produce 'right' answers.
(4)   Further distancing from peers, socially, intellectually. A growing lack of realism in her own self concept which is very low. Over-dependency on her from her parents who provide a poor social role model. Over-dependency on her need to achieve to get pleasure from herself and her work.
(5)   The need to step back. Opportunities for Elizabeth to take part in activities away from home. The teachers' response to her anger/frustration when she meets with criticism or comment. How they might help her respond more positively.
(6)   Joint plan of action in response to challenging tasks.
(7)   Joint planning on open-ended creative activities to take place out of school. The parents need counselling as well, as they appear to be trotting behind Elizabeth and not alongside her. She needs a healthy dose of common sense, given in an adult friendly way as she has the ability to understand sound explanations. I have met children who are quite shocked when confronted with the consequences of their behaviour in a friendly context and not a disciplinary one which tends to happen.

## Adolescent: Martin, aged 14

*Background information*

Martin is considered to be a 'walking disaster' by his teachers. He seems to live in a world of his own. He is never where he should be, and is invariably late for classes. He had great difficulties with the early stages of reading and writing, and never mastered the intricacies of spelling. His handwriting is appalling, and he is reluctant to put pen to paper. He has a very sharp wit and has become the class clown.

He was quite interested in school in the first two years. He had enjoyed the wide range of subjects. Last year things began to go wrong for him. He found teachers to be more concerned with maintaining their authority than in the pursuit of truth. He found the option system, moving into set syllabuses, very frustrating since there were fewer opportunities for 'theorising' and 'playing' with ideas.

His relationships with most teachers are extremely poor, since he tends to challenge and question both their authority and their knowledge. He is also rather dismissive of the views of many of his peers. His science teachers, however, value his contribution to class discussion, since he shows remarkable insight and understanding, beyond that of most young people of his age. He would like to devote himself exclusively to science, and science-related subjects, and dispense with the rest. He should be capable of achieving good examination results, were his present attitude and ability to present his work to change.

Martin is in a difficult phase at home. He is argumentative and restless. He is hopelessly untidy, and often unkind to his young sister. He is angry at his parents' accusations that he is lazy, and claims that when he is spending long periods watching TV he is in fact working hard in his head.

One is tempted to ask what does Martin get out of life in school!

*Points for discussion*

(1) What are the main issues for the school in helping Martin through the current phase?
(2) What could the school do through its organisation to ease the present difficulties?
(3) What might individual teachers do to improve their relationships with Martin?
(4) What help might you want from elsewhere, and how might such help be woven into what goes on in the school?
(5) What help do you want from the parents?
(6) What help could the school offer to the parents?

*Suggestions to help Martin*

Martin is a good example to show that the problems are nothing to do with his ability. He is just one of the unlucky adolescents in personal and emotional trouble.

(1)  Providing opportunities for Martin to express his ideas in class without this being damaging to other pupils' and teacher's morale. Persuading him to accept some help with work presentation without damaging his ego. Drama activities would probably help. Finding a way to help him become more self-organised, which he is willing to work on. Getting a negotiated agreement with him on his behaviour, and his commitment to work.

The dropping standards is a worrying sign.

cf: Main issue is to get Martin to believe he is being taken seriously, that school recognises his difficulties and dilemmas, acknowledges his abilities and welcomes them, and wants to find a *positive* solution.

(2)  Find him a 'personal' tutor with whom he would meet regularly to set up action plans on different aspects of his work and behaviour with regular reviews. Case conference with his teachers and him to agree on approaches to assessing his work, agree on policy for commenting/insisting on presentation criteria. Agree policy and process for him to negotiate some of his work, i.e. decisions on homework, assignments. Are there responsibilities in school for which he would contribute?

(3)  Discuss honestly with him the dilemma he places on his teachers. Get some agreement or a contract on how he will manage classroom discussion, and how teachers will provide him with respect too. Ask him how he wants his work assessed and to provide commentary for his own work. Get him to set his own targets.

(4)  Consultations with psychologist might help in discussions about how to get away from being the class clown and how to become more organised. Contacts with other local resources, college interest groups for enrichment possibilities.

(5)  Regular discussions with parents to present joint approach. Identification of areas where parental support/supervision could be helpful without damaging Martin's self-esteem.

(6)  A non-judgemental, supportive dialogue. A confident, positive stance towards Martin.

### Frances, aged 6½

Frances is the elder of our two children. Her younger brother, Joseph is 3½ years old. As a baby she slept little by day, but settled down fairly well at night.

Frances has always been demanding of our time, in the sense that she has always insisted on participating in every activity however unsuitable for a baby or toddler! Additionally she showed very little interest in the company of other children until she started school, and preferred the company of adults.

Even as a baby Frances was fascinated by books and language and seemed to possess a 'drive' to read. She achieved this around $2\frac{1}{2}$–3 years, and still reads voraciously. Frances has now settled happily at school. After a year in the reception class she jumped an academic year and then began to mix more easily with other children, although at times she still prefers her own company. Today Frances get enormous pleasure from playing chess, singing in the choir and learning the recorder, all activities she has taken up this year at school.

At home Frances can still be restless and excitable but will settle down with single-minded determination if something captures her interest, or an adult will play chess with her or present her with a page of sums to complete!

Frances has always been an affectionate child, although fairly volatile when crossed. She loathes being in the wrong, and can get very upset when things are not going smoothly. Fortunately her brother has a more phlegmatic approach to life and they get on well together.

Our main concern is that we feel she is frustrated by the slow pace of some lessons at schools and we feel she is underachieving. She seems to do so much of the same especially in mathematics.

# CHAPTER 3

# *Identification*

An instrument has been developed in advance of the needs of its possessor.
(Alfred Wallace)

It is the only example of evolution providing a species with an organ which it does not know how to use; a luxury organ, which will take its owner thousands of years to learn to put to proper use – if it ever does!     (Arthur Koestler)

The discussion of talented and gifted children is essentially linked with the need to develop suitable identification techniques and procedures which a busy teacher can use in the classroom. Because we have now accepted a broad definition, therefore children can be gifted or talented in various areas, then it is not surprising that many sources of information are typically used to identify this population of children. But essentially, these can be categorised into three major areas: teacher appraisal of their children, the use of rating scales and the administration of different types of standardised tests.

## Teacher appraisal of children

Obviously good professional teachers should know their children. They play the most important part in the identification of gifted and talented students. As a first step, the head teacher and the staff of the school should ask themselves the following simple questions. Do we have the best possible system for assessing, recording and communicating the needs of each child accurately, and are these records accessible to teachers and passed on from year to year group? The new National Curriculum and its assessment methodology should help considerably in this respect. There is a need for a system to be established for the clear recording of pupil's achievements and progress.

In the secondary stage of education, where more than one teacher is responsible for recording progress, a system should have built into it

27

procedures for collating all the information about the child into one single record. There should also be a suitable procedure set up for the regular and frequent exchange of information between teachers who are contributing to the total record. On p. 133 readers will find a suggested Referral Form and a method of recording observations of these children. It is essential that exceptional performance in any one subject should be known to teachers of other subjects so that disparities and underachievement may be considered. Ogilvie (1973) suggests that the teacher's subjective assessment of a pupil can be inaccurate if there is a tendency to rate most highly those pupils who are persevering, conforming, tidy and industrious. Many gifted pupils are careless, untidy and reluctant to write, since their speed of thinking is faster than their recording skills. It is, therefore, quite easy to mark a child down because of the poor quality of writing produced, but teachers need to give time and be patient to look at the underlying vocabulary and knowledge. This process of identification consists of making assessments and judgements. It must therefore, perforce contain a subjective and objective element. Any form of identification can be seen to lie on a continuum between these two areas.

There are certain broad principles which a teacher should consider when trying to identify these children: firstly, ensure that the process of identification is rooted in areas that the child is being allowed to experience; secondly, ensure that the child can express himself and listen carefully; and thirdly, ensure that the process of identification points towards useful developments and extension of the child's work.

Although a teacher is extremely busy with a multiplicity of jobs to fulfil, a professional teacher will try to screen the children and this relies heavily on teacher referral. It is obviously easier to do this in the primary sector, where teachers will probably teach the whole class for a whole year at a time, unlike a specialist teacher in the secondary phase, who may teach perhaps 300 different children in one week and therefore, it is extremely difficult to really know the children. Contrary to this Coleman (1985) found that teachers had more difficulty identifying younger children than older secondary level children. In addition, Howley et al. (1986) found that the more mixed the ethnic and racial composition of the class, the more difficult it was for a teacher to identify giftedness. Denton and Postlethwaite (1985) undertook an interesting piece of research on the effectiveness of testing secondary children in four subject areas and comparing this with teacher-based identification. This was carried out in a number of comprehensive schools in Oxfordshire. Teachers were more effective at identifying children in Mathematics and English than in Physics and French (see Table 3.1). It is interesting that the school which showed the closest match in English was also the school which showed the worst match in Physics.

This may reflect the difference between teacher-based and test-based judgement and may be due to teacher variation rather than of the impact of

Table 3.1: Overall percentages of test identified pupils which were also identified by teacher. Number of pupils in brackets.

| School | English | French | Physics | Maths |
|---|---|---|---|---|
| All schools | 61 (213) | 51 (210) | 45 (216) | 61 (215) |
| Range of % | 33–75 | 25–73 | 17–75 | 36–78 |

different school size, type or organisation. It is interesting to compare these figures with the results obtained by Pegnato and Birch (1959). They asked teachers to nominate children who were 'mentally gifted' and matched these nominations against those who scored 136 or more on an individually administered Stanford–Binet IQ test. They found that teachers identified 45 per cent of those who were above this IQ. They applied seven criteria, including teacher appraisal to identify gifted students. They found that teachers only refer 45 per cent of those identified as gifted. They also found that approximately 31 per cent of those identified by the teacher had average IQs. We should note, however, that there were some limitations in this research in that IQ was the only criteria used to determine giftedness, and it is possible that the teachers were using some other attribute as their criteria. Both Denton and Postlethwaite (1985) and Gear (1978) state that in-service training could help teachers in their assessment of such children. Gear noted that trained teachers correctly identified approximately 86 per cent, whereas the untrained correctly identified only 40 per cent. It was shown that the trained teachers helped eliminate some of the ambiguity about the nature of giftedness.

Teachers should also record their direct experience of pupils. This should provide a systematic record of their observation of the pupil's current behaviour, aptitudes and interests. Observation recording of skills does not come naturally. It would, therefore, be helpful to have a structured framework within which such observations can be formulated (see Tables 5.1 and 5.2).

In addition to teachers identifying from their own personal knowledge of their children, it is also essential that teachers should provide the creative learning environment where children have the opportunity to show their gifts and talents.

By the creative learning environment, one means a classroom in which thinking is valued far more than memory and in which the child expects to make a contribution that is valued and respected. It is also a classroom where the teacher supports and reinforces unusual ideas of children. Where failure is seen as a possible opportunity to help students realise errors and meet acceptable standards. A teacher adapts the classroom procedures to the student's interests and ideas wherever possible. This also means allowing time for students to think about developing their creative ideas in a climate of mutual respect and acceptance. This means a delicate balance between psychological safety and freedom, so that pupils are prepared to take risks. This balance also means freedom to think and to be adventurous, but not the behavioural freedom which leads to chaos. Such a teacher encourages divergent learning activities as well as listening and laughing with the students.

The teacher is the facilitator, the resource manager, the enthusiast, the guide, the prompter, the change agent. The teacher provides a warm, supportive atmosphere and allows children to make choices and to be a part of the decision making process. Such a teacher is not the only authority with the one right answer, because no-one can possibly know all there is to know about any one subject. However, it is unfortunate that there is still a great number of non-creative classrooms where there is little freedom to explore, the teacher is authoritarian, rigid and obsessed with keeping order. Teachers are unwilling to give individuals time and are insensitive to pupils' emotional needs.

It is important that a close relationship exists between the concept of giftedness, characteristics of gifted and talented children, identification and programmes of learning for them. Increasingly, identification should be viewed as a part of good teaching, a continuous process that anticipates further challenging learning experiences with a quality end product. Seen that way identification is an evaluation process that teachers undertake in the classroom, rather than a series of tests administered by outside specialists. That is not to deny that check lists and standardised achievement tests do not have their place.

I am indebted to Dr Don McAlpine for a copy of his excellent lecture to NZAGC (1991) in which he states:

> The so-called 'responsive environment' approach to the identification of these children contains many advantages. First of all, it offers more professional responsibility to teachers to assess children's abilities. Secondly, teachers become more interested in the programme if they are also involved in the identification. Thirdly, identification is embedded naturally into the day to day learning and teaching activities of the regular classroom. The general quality of teaching for *all* children is thereby improved. The gifted programme is not an oasis in a desert, but the whole classroom is an oasis. Fourthly, identification becomes closely linked to objectives of the programme. Identification should always be seen as a means to an end and never as an end in itself.

What are some of the limitations of the responsive environment approach? The quality of teachers is very uneven in respect to methods of iden-tification, in the use of tests and other evaluation techniques. There are, therefore, threats to reliability and validity in the identification process. As a result, some children may be overlooked while others, for example teacher-pleasers, may be included. With large classes in a mainstreamed context, it is yet another task to perform with a consequent increase in workload and commitment to the programme which must follow. Finally, teachers with indifferent and negative attitudes to the gifted and talented children may do nothing at all to identify or cater for such children.

## Exercise: myths and misconceptions

(1) It is suggested that you should read through the following lists and check which items are misconceptions.

(2) Tick which three you agree with the most and star those you disagree with and consider to be a myth.

(3) Think of the most gifted and talented child you know and circle which items apply to that particular individual.

I am indebted to Richard Lange and Mark German for giving me permission to use the following list.

## Characteristics of gifted learners

Gifted children:

- have everything going their way
- are more emotionally stable and mature than their non-gifted peers
- prefer to work alone
- are model students
- always reveal their giftedness
- are organised and neat
- are well-rounded
- are creative
- are good learners
- are very verbal
- have good handwriting
- are good spellers
- have very supportive parents and come from good homes
- have a low tolerance for slower students
- are perfectionists
- work harder than average kids
- look or act differently

## Identification procedures

- gifted students always reveal their intelligence
- gifted students are respected and looked up to by their peers
- Asians tend to have the highest percentage of gifted students
- gifted handicapped students are best served within the special education environment

- highly gifted children become socially maladjusted
- gifted children can no more be stopped from achieving their potential than a cannonball can be diverted from its path once it has been fired
- girls appear with much greater frequency than boys do in gifted programmes
- culturally diverse gifted students have a great difficulty fitting into traditional programmes for the gifted
- non-identified siblings feel left out

Identification procedures should include these items:

- IQ testing
- test scores, achievement
- parent inventory
- self inventory
- staff inventory/checklist
- student grades/report cards
- student products
- subjective teacher comments

*Programme models and delivery systems*

- gifted students need constant challenges
- teachers prefer to work with gifted students
- double promotion can be harmful to gifted students
- gifted programmes should be a reward to gifted students
- teachers of gifted students should be gifted themselves
- gifted classes end up with the best teachers
- gifted students learn things with only one presentation
- total segregation is the best model
- pull-out programmes cause double-duty
- mentorship programmes are not worth the effort it takes to organise

There follows a variety of methods for identifying gifted and talented children covering the major talent areas. Some children show themselves as very able by their high energy or intense curiosity, others are more difficult to spot and deliberately hide their talents. A multi-dimensional, integrated approach is therefore necessary. More emphasis is put on areas where there has been less research, recognition and application in the classroom starting with a question, action and purpose exercise.

# Identification procedure

Initial concern from parents, teacher or pupil that a pupil may be exceptionally able or talented and that their curriculum needs may not be being fully met.

| Question | Action | Purpose |
|---|---|---|

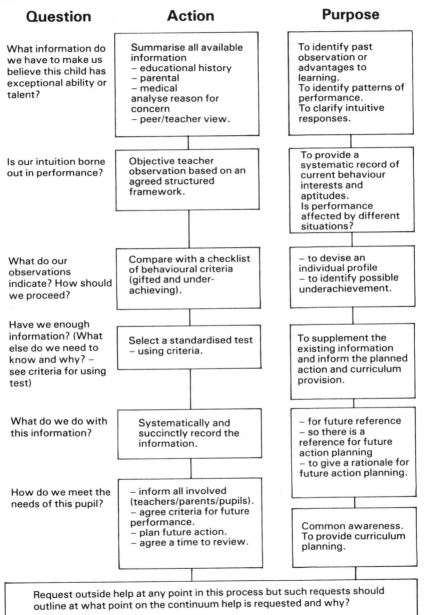

| Question | Action | Purpose |
|---|---|---|
| What information do we have to make us believe this child has exceptional ability or talent? | Summarise all available information<br>– educational history<br>– parental<br>– medical<br>analyse reason for concern<br>– peer/teacher view. | To identify past observation or advantages to learning.<br>To identify patterns of performance.<br>To clarify intuitive responses. |
| Is our intuition borne out in performance? | Objective teacher observation based on an agreed structured framework. | To provide a systematic record of current behaviour interests and aptitudes.<br>Is performance affected by different situations? |
| What do our observations indicate? How should we proceed? | Compare with a checklist of behavioural criteria (gifted and under-achieving). | – to devise an individual profile<br>– to identify possible underachievement. |
| Have we enough information? (What else do we need to know and why? – see criteria for using test) | Select a standardised test<br>– using criteria. | To supplement the existing information and inform the planned action and curriculum provision. |
| What do we do with this information? | Systematically and succinctly record the information. | – for future reference<br>– so there is a reference for future action planning<br>– to give a rationale for future action planning. |
| How do we meet the needs of this pupil? | – inform all involved (teachers/parents/pupils).<br>– agree criteria for future performance.<br>– plan future action.<br>– agree a time to review. | Common awareness.<br>To provide curriculum planning. |

Request outside help at any point in this process but such requests should outline at what point on the continuum help is requested and why?

## Intelligence and its assessment

> Intelligence can only come when there is freedom – freedom to think, to observe, to question.
> (Krishnamurti)

One of the most controversial and yet fascinating aspects of education is intelligence. Intelligence has been defined as the ability to see relationships and to use this ability to solve problems. Some psychologists facetiously define intelligence as the ability to do intelligence tests! A problem of definition has burdened psychologists since Cicero coined the word 'intelligentia' based on ideas used by both Aristotle and Plato.

From the above definition, we can see that all children's formal work in school can be influenced by the outcome of intelligence testing. In addition, high or low intelligence can carry important vocational and social significance for our children. In many countries the bottom-line instrument for confirming suspected high ability is an individual intelligence test.

The other area of controversy is the continuing debate as to whether intelligence is inherited or determined by environmental factors. The author finds it impossible to conceive that intellectual superiority can be attributed to any one factor, whether it is environmental, genetic or neurological. Clark (1983) maintains that gifted children have different neurological and biochemical makeup and Sternberg (1989) gives an equally convincing argument asserting that intelligence is determined by the amount, type and degree of environmental stimulation that a child receives including the quality of the environment and the attitudes of parents.

Academic ability is probably the major reason why gifted children are identified initially, as such children perform well in academic subjects but are also persistent, well instructed and have good study skills. These children also often do well in intelligence tests because they process information quickly, have better memories, greater accuracy and are good at abstract thinking.

However, not all gifted children have these attributes, as some have difficulty in mastering basic skills. This is why this book emphasises a multi-dimensional approach to identification and support. It is little wonder, therefore, that both parents and teachers take a great deal of interest in it, but at the same time, there are many misconceptions as to its measurements and significance which can affect a child's progress.

The most common tests of intelligence used by educational psychologists are: The Wechsler Intelligence Scale for Children (WISC-R UK) and the British Ability Scale (BAS). These tests comprise a range of separate subtests from which an Intelligent Quotient (IQ) can be calculated. When David Wechsler put together the subtests of the WISC he identified subtests that were felt to be measures of some of the underlying abilities related to school achievement. His choice of subtest was to some extent arbitrary but a consideration of the statistical data available in the WISC Manual, indicates that the subtests correlate between 0.3 and 0.5 which is modest but acceptable. However, it has been observed that there are a number of tests, for example, tests of mechanical ability which were found not to correlate with the other items of the WISC and which were therefore rejected. For practitioners who would value information about the whole range of a child's abilities this somewhat ruthless selection of subtests was unfortunate, though the core subtests available provide a reasonable range with which to obtain the profile of a child's skills. The BAS designed by Colin Elliot and others, contains a much wider selection of subtests and therefore for some age groups can enable the psychologist to build up a more accurate profile of skills and abilities. These tests, unlike the earlier IQ tests which were predominantly objective items requiring one right answer, have higher subjective contents with more sophisticated methods of interpretation. These provide the best consensus test to date, but there is still much to be learnt regarding what tests really test in the light of the ever changing theory of intelligence. These tests include two major types: group attainments tests which can be useful indicators of ability; and individual tests, open to teachers, which are designed to reveal levels of cognitive ability and potential, these require considerable time and expertise for their administration and, therefore, should be undertaken by an educational psychologist. Such tests may be administered, for example, shortly after pupils enter a school or college, or when there is concern at underachievement. However, problems can arise. There is a need for staff to be aware of the purposes for which the tests are to be used, to know how to interpret the results and to recognise the limitations of such tests. Additionally, there is a need to counter the probability of early categorisation and labelling of pupils and self-fulfilling prophecies. Some aspects and forms of high ability do not lend themselves to standardised testing, which additionally limits the value of such tests.

In doubtful cases, schools should contact their educational psychologist who will be able to offer more detailed and accurate assessment and advice. While it may be the case that an intelligence test may have been designed under the misapprehension that intelligence is a unitary concept, this does not preclude its use in a more flexible way to build up a cognitive profile. It is only to be expected that the mean scores that children obtain on intelligence tests subscales increase as the child's age increases.

'Viewing mind' from an entirely different perspective, Sternberg and Davidson (1986) considered the development of giftedness – the development of children with markedly greater intellectual achievements than is common. Sternberg, in pursuing his speculations on excellence may have been able to highlight factors that have not previously been apparent. He identified three factors in the genesis of giftedness: 'Intelligence, Creativity and Commitment'. He felt that gifted children might be expected to score well on broadly based intelligence tests such as the WISC and that a high score on the WISC was in some way a pre-requisite for high levels of achievement, but by no means a sufficient feature.

**Table 3.2**

| Typical IQ test questions | Typical creativity test questions |
|---|---|
| 1. Glove is to hand as shoe is to . . . | What would happen if everyone was born with three fingers and no thumb? |
| 2. What is a bucket? | How many uses can you think of for a bucket? |
| 3. If a girl goes into a shop and buys 37p of sweets and gives the man 50p, how much change will she get back? | How many different ways can you think of to get an answer of 7? |

Creativity was included as one of his three factors, because he felt that in order to be able to think originally or to see or understand things that others do not, a child would need to challenge the prevailing and conceptual frameworks and as it were, stand outside the conventional ways of looking at things.

There appear to be children who have aptitude for creativity as apart from academic aptitude. Indeed, there is no correlation between the two after a threshold IQ of 100 (Ogilvie, 1973). These children are often referred to as being divergent thinkers and educationalists frequently use the Guilford model of fluency, originality, flexibility and foresight, as opposed to convergent thinking, which emphasises the more traditional academic skills such as memory, classification and reasoning ability. Some distinctions can be seen in Table 3.2 where the IQ questions only have one correct answer, whereas the creativity questions stress the importance of many answers. Creativity is discussed in more detail later.

The dispute concerning the relative independence of intelligence and creativity still exists.

Perhaps intelligence of IQ 100 plus is the best predictor of academic achievement, but above this point increases of creativity become more significant for the prediction of the achievement of some children. This is generally seen to be a feature of creativity though by no means a sufficient characteristic. The third factor that Sternberg identified, 'commitment' was seen as a very significant feature because he felt that it was only with great motivation and indeed, dedication and sacrifice, that the creative gifts of adults become apparent and that it is only with strong motivation that children are able to achieve in school or in an academic situation. Renzulli (1977) also included commitment as an essential factor in gifted achievement. It is by identifying commitment as an essential ingredient in very high achievement that both Sternberg and Renzulli have identified a factor that helps us to make sense of intelligence and cognitive profiles.

The consistent feature of much of our understanding of intelligence is that those human characteristics which in Western growth oriented economics confer personal and social advantages are the characteristics most closely associated with the notion of intelligence. People who can manage a company efficiently or succeed in their chosen profession are invariably thought of by others as intelligent. It may be therefore that our understanding of the mix of skills and abilities that constitute intelligence is a feature of the social objectives and values that we share in Western society. In other societies the mix of abilities which enable a person to find water in the most severe desert conditions or to make an accurate blowpipe could equally well be regarded as a hallmark of an intelligent person always supposing that their language had an equivalent concept. It is possible using modern psychometric measures to identify the cognitive profiles that are associated with success in different professions and in different cultures, without necessarily putting a value judgement on those profiles and declaring that one is somehow better than another. Unfortunately the present generation of psychometric tests do not enable the psychologist to build up more than a rough and ready profile on which broader decisions might be made. The current difficulties with profiling would appear to reside in the limitations of the subtests that comprise the separate batteries. When subtests are designed they have to be easily administered and should not take too long to complete, otherwise there would be a risk of mal-administration of the test and long drawn out tests would be likely to fatigue anyone taking them and lead to an invalid estimate of test performance. The standardisation of tests is a long and expensive procedure and it takes many years to prepare a reliable measure. It has in consequence taken many years to prepare the present BAS. The material of the tests rapidly becomes dated and so test producers are hard pressed to maintain the validity of the tests they have already published, let alone develop new ones. The limitations on the subtests and the vast labour involved in their standardisation has limited the availability of broad measures of intelligence, such as the WISC, the BAS, and in many cases research has been carried out using simple paper and pencil tests. These are typically of the form where people have to identify which of a collection of items is not part of the group, complete a sequence or construct a word from a pattern or a sequence of letters. While there is a correlation between results of these tests and the aggregate scores of the broad range measures of intelligence, unlike the broad range tests they do not yield a cognitive profile. As we have seen, an isolated IQ score cannot of itself offer much information since the meaning of the tests resides in the profile constructed from the results.

*School achievement and giftedness*

If a child has the right balance of abilities to achieve well in an academic setting, what significance does this have for the child? A distinction has often been made between high achieving children in a school situation, referred to as 'schoolhouse gifted' by Renzulli (1977), and creativity in older adults in the field of say, mathematics, engineering or the arts. It has been proposed that the abilities necessary for higher school achievement, often in the form of nine GCSEs at Grade A, are quite different to the ability needed to make significant contribution to research or an outstanding achievement in the arts. Attention has been drawn to the differing conditions in which 'schoolhouse giftedness' and creative adult achievement take place. School achievement is the result of hard work in a wide range of differing areas of the curriculum where the level of study is fairly superficial and the problems that need to be solved are normally quite clearly defined. On the other hand adult creative achievement is usually the result of single minded dedication, often extending over many years, to the resolution of problems that are usually vague and quite undefined. It should not come as any surprise to find that many adults that have a proven record of high creative, academic achievement, do not score especially well on paper and pencil measures of intelligence. Indeed, intelligence tests are based on tasks with clearly defined problems and answers that are either right or wrong. No satisfactory tests has yet been prepared that can measure a person's ability to resolve ill-defined problems with no clearly correct or incorrect solutions. For example, before it became possible to solve some mathematical problems, it was essential to invent specific mathematical techniques for doing so. The incentive needed for the creative invention was the need to solve a physical or mathematical problem, but the invention of the technique itself, for example Calculus complex numbers, non-Euclidian geometry, was a purely creative act. While there have been no tests yet devised to measure this kind of ability, there have been attempts. Getzels and Jackson (1962) devised specific tests of creativity. These were of the form 'how many uses can you think of for a box of chocolates, a dead cat, a sleeping child' etc. This style of assessment of creativity is included in the current BAS as a subtest, but these tests can only be scored by totting up the number of distinct uses identified, and little regard can be given to the quality of the responses. It is a matter of personal opinion, at the present time, whether these tests really reflect a relevant dimension of creativity.

## The educational implications of tests and cognitive profiles

The application of intelligence testing to everyday classroom practice has been more successful in the area of identifying children's strengths and cognitive weaknesses. Educational programmes can be designed which match the cognitive profile of a child in such a way that areas of success can be guaranteed where there are known strengths and programmes can be very carefully constructed in areas in which the child is weak to ensure also that there is success in these areas. Testing has been used for some time to identify underachievement, but again the profiling approach can help teachers to be more specific about the areas in which underachievement is likely and can alert them to the specific needs of children in those areas. Underlying much of the interpretation of test results, have been Information Processing models of mental structure. It should be possible at some stage, by carefully considering the components of educational tasks such as reading, to match aspects of the educational task to a child's cognitive profile and thereby explain high achievement or specific difficulty. At present it is possible to design educational programmes which take into account the evident weaknesses of children in specific skill areas. Information processing models focus on the role of short-term as opposed to long-term memory, the encoding and decoding of linguistic information as well as the broader aspects of the flexibility of concept formation and inspection times. At the present stage of our knowledge however, an interpretation of cognitive profiles and an appreciation of the associated education difficulties cannot be made by any simple deductive approach but relies on long standing educational and clinical experience. Standing by themselves the test results are only of limited value. At the present time too, tests take very little account of attention skill deficits and observations about these cannot be easily integrated into assessment findings. At the present stage of our knowledge the assessment of intelligence appears to be in part scientific and in part intuition.

## Creativity

Creativity is now firmly established as one of the significant categories associated with giftedness and talent, and is one of the terms used in our broad definition. With the widening of the concept to include creativity and other abilities, giftedness has become a multi-category concept. However, we should remind ourselves that this has not always been so, and that in early studies of the gifted, creativity did not feature in this way. Intelligence, rather narrowly defined, was the sole criterion. However, we should note that few programmes around the world emphasised creativity as the focal point of gifted programming or identification. Too little emphasis is placed on the development of creativity in all gifted students and even less significance is placed on identifying creatively gifted students. For those who hold on to the narrow definition, they will leave significant numbers of creatively gifted students out of programmes for the gifted and talented. In addition, we should remember that some of the greatest strengths of disadvantaged and culturally different students are their creative skills and motivations.

At a time when charges of elitism are often aimed at programmes for the gifted, and the very word 'gifted' serves as a red flag in some communities, parents and educators could do far worse than to consider the positive and beneficial impact that programmes centred on creativity and the creative talent development might have in their respective communities.

One of the problems which surface when we explore the role creativity plays in the gifted population involves identification. Nearly everyone recognises, or knows what creativity is, generally, but there is less agreement on precise definitions and identification instruments. It is suspected that most of us in education use the word every day without considering its real meaning.

Researchers such as Torrance (1962) and Getzels and Jackson (1962), who have accepted the more broadened construct of giftedness, are paying more attention to the importance of imaginative or creative thinking as a major contributor to innovative thought and responsive knowledge production. Most of the psychometric research on gifted populations is primarily concerned with academic achievement or convergent intellectual potentialities, while research on creativity frequently holds a more secondary status, possible because of its lack of theory and assessment schemes. Professor Ned Herrmann in his excellent lecture to the 7th World Conference on gifted and talented children (1987) highlighted the need to take creativity far more seriously, link the creative brain to mental wholeness, personal uniqueness, change and productivity, which are just a few of the important parameters of creativity and giftedness. Nurturing of this important mental potentiality should not only be seen in the context of differentiated teaching, but also more general terms, by utilising it in society at large, and in education generally. By including children with this particular talent area, we have therefore had a broadening effect on attitudes towards the gifted and is partly responsible for the reduction of elitism for which we are often charged. Its inclusion has also made an impact on both the curriculum and on the nature of teaching generally, for a wide range of children in the classroom.

Urban (1988) states that high creativity is seen as the ability to create a new, unusual and surprising product by perceiving, processing and utilising a maximum of available information; by association, combining and composing this information with data from experienced or imagined elements and data; by synthesising all parts or elements into a theme or holistic Gestalt in whatever shape or form; and, lastly by communicating and sharing the creative product with others. McAlpine (1988) states that some consideration of creativity as the resolution of conflict and the fusion of thinking, feeling, sensing and intuition, helps to eliminate our understanding of creative thinking. Wallace (1986) states that creativity is a resolution of conflict and reminds us that Jung saw creativity as 'the balance between the conscious and the sub-conscious, the rational and the irrational, extroversion and introversion, divergent and convergent'. Vaughan (1977) also sees creativity as a delicate balancing of opposites which produces a new integration or synthesis. A creative process can only be maintained by holding the opposites in a state of dynamic tension.

Clark (1983) has elaborated an integrated model of creativity consisting of four major dimensions: (i) thinking; (ii) feeling; (iii) intuition; (iv) sensing. The thinking aspect involves sensing and solving problems and the use of divergent thinking abilities. Children make sense of their world by using their senses and our primary school colleagues use this aspect admirably. The feeling aspect focuses on emotional wellbeing and self-actualising. By this means comes an attitude of mind – if you think well of yourself you can meet your creative potential. Thirdly, the intuitive component employs imagery, fantasy and impulses to assist breakthroughs to the pre-conscious and unconscious states. This is very much a right brain activity. Educationalists should be aware that children need to be encouraged in this area, because our educational system is biased towards the left brain (Blakeslee, 1980). While creativity in the arts can often function well with little help from the variable left brain processes, most creative work requires a healthy co-operation between intuition and logical thought.

If we put theory aside for a moment and look at the real world of people who have proved to be truly great, then Mozart is a most topical example in his bi-centenary year. He described his apparently sub-conscious process of musical composition in a famous letter.

> When I feel well and in good humour, or when I am taking a drive or walking after a good meal, or in the night when I cannot sleep, thoughts crowd into my mind as easily as you could wish. Whence and how do they come? I do not know, and I have nothing to do with. Those which please me I keep in my mind and hum them; at least others tell me that I do so. Once I have my theme, another melody comes linking itself to the first one, in accordance with the needs of the composition as a whole: the counterpoint, the part of each instrument, and all those melodic fragments at last produce the entire work.

The sensing attribute involves a high level of mental and physical development resulting in inventions and products in talent areas. However, McAlpine (1988) suggests that three caveats should be noted: (i) not all creative thinkers exhibit all of the traits mentioned; (ii) in themselves these characteristics of thinking and cognitive style do not guarantee creativity – they are pre-dispositions or enabling attributes; (iii) they may have different faces and forms for different age groups.

*Creativity test*

It is quite revealing to ask children to write down as many uses of a certain object, such as a brick, bucket or a newspaper. In this case, a nine year old girl made this list in just ten minutes. This shows fluency and a divergent-thinking child.

**Uses of a newspaper**: 1. read it; 2. use as a tablecloth; 3. make paper hats with it; 4. draw funny faces on it; 5. make paper aeroplanes; 6. make paper people; 7. make collage; 8. make paper wallets; 9. screw up for use as a projectile; 10. fill in football results; 11. do the crossword; 12. cut out the photographs from it; 13. make dress patterns of it; 14. make a kite with it; 15. make a fire with it; 16. use it as wrapping paper; 17. wrap up fish and chips in it etc., etc.

The term 'creativity' then is an extremely difficult concept to define and subsequently, to measure. The term has multiple meanings and can be defined quite differently by different people (Klein, 1982). However, to many teachers, it may be quite apparent which students are highly creative and which are not.

In connection with a more broadened construct of giftedness (Torrance, 1966; Getzels and Jackson, 1962), researchers are paying more and more attention to the importance of imaginative or creative thinking as a major contributor to innovative thought and socially responsible as well as responsive knowledge production. Most of the psychometric research on gifted populations is primarily concerned with academic achievement or convergent intellectual potentialities, while research on creativity frequently holds more secondary status due to its uncertain theory and assessment schemes. There is a need to take creativity more seriously and link the 'creative brain' to mental wholeness, personal uniqueness, change and productivity, which are just a few of the important parameters of creativity and giftedness.

The nurture of this important mental potentiality should not only be seen in the context of 'differential education for the gifted' but also in more general terms by utilising it in society at large and education in general, regardless of developmental levels or ideologies.

One of the most important pre-conditions required for creativity to be unleashed is the adequate identification of high, average or low creative potentials so parental, educational, and/or political intervention can reinforce, redirect, revise or even enhance creativity.

> Even though there are already many screening devices on the market, we had reasons to design a more culture-sensitive instrument that assesses creative potentials in most age and ability groups from various educational, socio-economic, and cultural backgrounds. We also wanted an instrument that was easy to administer, economical in time and cost with a set of evaluation criteria requiring minimal training. (Jellen and Urban, 1986)

Thus, the test should provide the testees with a basic set of information which can be used by them in every creative way possible. But in order to get a high degree of culture-fairness, they decided to avoid verbal clues by choosing a drawing task instead, with certain figural stimuli. These figural fragments were intentionally designed in an incomplete fashion with no or only vague conventional meanings in order to achieve a maximum of flexibility as an imperative for creativity. The six differing fragments mirror diverse characteristics that are:

(1) different in design
(2) geometric and nongeometric
(3) round and straight
(4) singular and compositional
(5) broken and unbroken
(6) within and outside a given frame
(7) placed irregularly on the space provided
(8) incomplete.                                    (Urban and Jellen, 1986)

The outcome is the Test for Creative Thinking–Drawing Production or, in short, the TCT–DP (Jellan and Urban, 1989).

The first pilot studies revealed that the TCT–DP can indeed detect or identify high, average, as well as low creative potential in most age and ability groups. The subjects chosen for pilot testing came, however, exclusively from a German cultural background differing in types of schooling received or attended. These first findings were congruent with other research findings on creativity: (1) A moderate group correlation existed between the means of TCT–DP and the academic achievement level of the groups tested; (2) No correlation was seen between individual IQ scores and TCT–DP scores in a group of subjects of relatively homogeneous intellectual caliber. These positive findings with German samples verifying the validity and reliability of the instrument encouraged them to continue their research by breaking the ethnocentricity of the data base, inviting colleagues from around the world to co-operate in a cross-cultural application of the TCT–DP.

High creativity is seen as the ability to create a new, unusual and surprising product by perceiving, processing and utilising a maximum of available information; by associating, combining and composing this information with data from experience or imagined elements and data; by synthesising all parts or elements into a theme or holistic Gestalt in whatever shape or form; and lastly, by communicating or sharing the creative art/product with others (Urban, 1985).

Since practical activities without a theory base are unreliable, the researchers took as their definition of creativity 'the emergence in action of a novel product growing out of the uniqueness of the individual and the materials, events, people or circumstances of the person's life' (Rogers, 1962). The test allows each child to expand, extend, develop and create something that is unique and satisfying to the child and not necessarily the tester.

The eleven valuation criteria chosen for the test reflect on openness to experience and explore the six fragments in and outside the box. In order to avoid culture bias the researchers used only a drawing task with no verbal clues. The children are simply asked to complete the picture and give it a title.

The author tested 50 ten year old children and the most and least creative drawings are below. Readers may like to try assessing these based on the criteria above. Questions to consider:

(1)  Are there major differences between genders?
(2)  Can the test be applied to children from different countries and cultures?
(3)  What does the test tell us about children's creative ability?

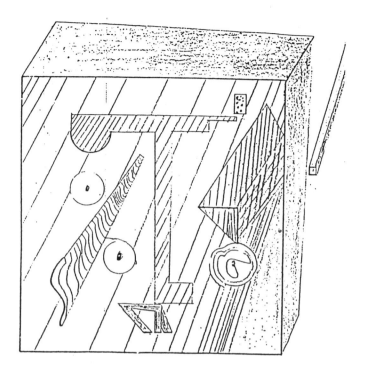

*A general identification check list*

Check lists have been developed to improve the efficiency of teacher judgement. They are rather subjective often poorly constructed and with no indication how well a child must score to be considered gifted.

They are not tests to determine whether or not a particular child is exceptionally able. Each child is unique, and any one child may or may not show some, all or none of the characteristics described. But check lists can prove helpful in alerting parents and teachers to the possibility that they may be midjudging some of their children and it would encourage them to look for signs or talents which they may have so far failed to acknowledge. They can influence strategies however, and can open up a dialogue with children and parents.

Many different check lists have been put forward, some fairly short and concise; others of great length and all embracing detail. More recently specific check lists have been devised for subject specialists at the secondary stage. The completed check list below attempts to include the most commonly mentioned features, without becoming unnecessarily complex.

None of these behaviours should be taken as proof of high ability but they can alert teachers and parents to the need to question the reasons for their occurrence. If a child measures up to quite a number of these listed

*A completed teacher's check-list showing the ability profile of a possibly gifted pupil*

| Child's Name: *Jane Smith* | | | Sex: *F* | Age: *9y 3m*  Date of Birth:  *03.04.81* | | |
|---|---|---|---|---|---|---|
| Characteristic | Poor | Weak | Average | Good | Exceptional |
| Use of language | | | | | x |
| Reasoning ability | | | | | x |
| Speed of thought | | | | | x |
| Imagination | | | | x | |
| Memory | | | | | x |
| Observation | | | | x | |
| Concentration | | | x | | |
| Whether questioning | | | | | x |
| Makes original suggestions | | | | x | |
| Problem solving | | | | | x |
| Extent of reading | | | | | x |
| Routine work | x | | | | |

This is typical in that the child is bored with routine work whereas other characteristics are clustered towards the exceptional end.

and Jane certainly does, then you should enquire further into a child's abilities.

## Psychomotor ability

The appeal of our definition is that it recognises not only high general intelligence, but also specific talent areas, including psychomotor skills. Terman's (1981) detailed studies of gifted children (Stanford–Binet IQs of 140 plus) showed them to be healthier and even better physical specimens, although the Americans have now excluded psychomotor ability on the grounds that artistic psychomotor talents such as dancing, could be included under the performing arts, and that students who are gifted and talented in sport were already well provided for. The author considers it is essential that all talent areas should be identified. Most schools do have good facilities for our athletes such as expensive sports halls, specialist trained physical education teachers, a considerable amount of individualised learning and a great deal of encouragement and reward. Indeed, the sports programmes in many of our schools could be exemplars of what a gifted programme should be.

In the DES document, Curriculum 5-16 (1985), Her Majesty's Inspectors state that curricula physical education should include five areas of experience to promote skilful body management. 'Participation in creative, artistic activities requiring expressive movement, competition between groups or individuals involving the use of psychomotor skills, activities leading to increased suppleness, mobility, strength and stamina; and challenging experiences in various environments.' This classification closely identifies with the description of sport offered in the European 'Sport for All' Charter (1976) linking physical education in schools with outside community agencies responsible for sport, dance and physical recreation generally.

This divide is important, because although we have reasonable facilities and well-trained teachers in physical education, the outside community facilities and encouragement from experts are very much a part of the extension necessary for our young people.

My own philosophy has been greatly influenced by the ideas of Carolyn Jones of Newcastle-upon-Tyne University, who deems the aims of physical education to be: firstly, the physical development of each person; secondly, the development of the whole person in society through physical activities; and thirdly, the promotion of excellence and life-long participation in physical activity. This philosophy respects, within the frameworth of society, the individuality of human growth and development and the uniqueness of each person. It is also a view which encapsulates what Parry (1977) refers to as 'qualitarianism' or excellence on the one hand and 'egalitarianism' or sport for all on the other. Each enriches the other and quality is the prize: quality in human endeavour; quality in education; and quality of life. This personal perspective receives some support from the DES.

> Provision of physical education, like that for other aspects of education, must be planned with the needs of all young people in mind. Every child should have the option to take part in sport at a level appropriate to his ability and existing resources should allow him that opportunity. (DES, 1978)

The Sports Council (1984) would suggest that it is not just a form of National and World Class Championships, for few attain these heights, but also encouragement for each individual to achieve their own level and fulfil their own potential. It also recognises that there are differential levels of achievement amongst individuals and that as a result, success in psychomotor ability is relative and is a matter of degree. This interpretation of the word 'excellence' incorporates the full ability range, as well as including all forms of psychomotor ability. This gets over the problem that some people feel that the concept of excellence should not be restricted to an elitist version which is equated with giftedness. The term has a wider application than this, for it is, we should affirm, a matter of developing in each person their physical skills to full potential.

If we then agree that one of the aims of physical education in our schools is the complete development of whole people, then we are agreed with the World Health Organisation's definition of health, which is a 'state of complete physical, mental and social well-being, not merely the absence of disease and infirmity'. We should go further and say that if we believe the healthy body equals a healthy mind, then we mean that physical education has a vital part in developing our young people with the power to live a full, adult, living breathing life in close contact with what I love. I want to be all that I am capable of becoming.

The tendency in education, and I suspect this could well increase, is to develop the cognitive areas of a child to the detriment of the cultural, physical and the spiritual dimensions. For example, there is a growing interest in the idea that we can all take more responsibility for our own health and a recognition that good health is more than freedom from disease or infirmity. The idea of a holistic living programme is now the fastest growing and most important development in the domain of health and healing. It is a programme of self-care in which a person is seen as a whole body, mind and spirit, with each part inter-related. Despite the tendency in schools for physical education to decline, we should strongly believe in the concept of a healthy mind and a healthy body and, therefore, PE needs protection and our support.

Some consideration is now called for in defining the area of psychomotor ability. The nature and range of physical skills, which we are concerned to develop in children have been well documented, and have been prescribed quite closely by the Physical Education Committee of HMI (1979). These skills include perception, decision making, control of movement, evaluation, physical skills, skills of posture and orientation, fine manipulative skills, gross motor skills, artistic skills and communication skills.

There are distinct areas of experience within the subject through which psychomotor confidence may be achieved. This has been identified as follows:

(1)   Areas in which the main aim is the development of skilful body management.
(2)   Areas in which the main aim is creating or being involved in an artistic experience through body movement.
(3)   Areas in which the main aim is competition between groups of individuals involving the use of psychomotor skills.
(4)   Areas in which the main aim is body training leading to increased powers of strength, stamina, endurance and a general feeling of well-being.

(5)   Areas in which the main aim is to meet challenging experience in changing environments.

Within these five areas of experience, activities should, therefore, be encouraged: gymnastics, games, athletics, swimming and general outdoor pursuits. The DES (1977) confirm Ogilvie's (1973) findings that the exceptional performer is easily identifiable by his or her achievements and that performance in many physical activities is quantifiable. However, the identification of outstanding potential is more problematic, possibly because of the following reasons:

(a)   The difficulties distinguished between early maturation and exceptional ability.
(b)   The problem of catering for the late developer.
(c)   The diversity of physical activities.
(d)   Psychomotor ability may be unitary or multi-faceted.
(e)   Psychomotor ability is dependent upon opportunity.

However, experienced teachers and others should be able to recognise the attributes of strength, endurance, supplety, agility, co-ordination, rhythm, harmonious movement, balance and economy of effort.

**Visual and performing arts**

This is an area of the curriculum which is under considerable pressure because the National Curriculum puts greater weight on English, Mathematics and Science which are largely left brain activities and yet, it is considered vitally important that the whole curriculum for the whole child should include these aesthetic areas of a child's education. Following are lists that characterise children with potential talents in Art, Drama and Music:

*Art*

(1)   Demonstrate vivid imagination.
(2)   Remember great detail.
(3)   Draw a great variety of things and not just flowers, houses and people.
(4)   Have a long attention span for these art activities, including planning the composition of their work well.
(5)   They are delighted to try out different materials, media and varying techniques.
(6)   Are keen observers of the world around them, but then this applies to scientists as well.
(7)   Set high standards of quality and often re-work their creation to achieve these ends.

(8) Take art activities very seriously and derive great satisfaction from them. This includes showing interest in other children's creations.

## Drama

(1) They are adept at improvising, imitation and role-play.
(2) They are often lithe, can handle their bodies well with ease and poise.
(3) They show great interest in dramatic activities and often volunteer for plays and sketches.
(4) They often relate stories with the effective use of gestures and facial expressions – watch their body language.
(5) They create original work.
(6) They can create suspense and easily relate stories which evoke emotional responses from their listeners.
(7) They can hold the attention of the class and get others to respond well.

## Music

(1) They obviously enjoy and seek out musical activities and take every opportunity to hear and create music
(2) They may play a musical instrument or express a strong desire to do so from the early years
(3) They often have perfect pitch
(4) They make up original tunes
(5) They can easily remember and produce melodies and rhythm patterns
(6) They are knowledgeable about background sounds, chords and individual instruments
(7) They respond sensitively to music by body movements and mood changes

## Leadership

Generally, students who are more articulate, better adjusted and more socially adaptable seem to be rated high on leadership qualities. Here are a few leadership roles:

1. Setting a good example
2. Controlling and unifying
3. Making policy
4. Good planning
5. Pooling and focusing ideas
6. Achieving a goal
7. Identifying a need
8. Providing expertise
9. Taking responsibility
10. Taking action
11. Encouraging the less able
12. Observant and sensitive to people
13. Having a sense of humour and making life enjoyable
14. A preference for innovation
15. Influencing other children's behaviour
16. Being rigorous and persistent
17. Self confidence and a good self concept

Plowman (1981) itemised six aspects of leadership in the form of adjectives which are: charismatic, intuitive, generative, analytical, evaluative and synergistic.

From the list of characteristics above, the reader can see that the list could be categorised under cognitive, affective, or indeed, both.

Chapter 4 will include leadership education. We can teach children to learn about the characteristics of leadership, how to be a good leader, as well as placing them in leadership situations in order to enhance this particular talent area.

### Recognising talent by the quality of work children produce

Possibly the best way to recognise high ability in any aspect of the school work is the actual performance of children. Several examples of children's work follow, covering different subjects and ages of children.

There are at least two questions both parents and teachers should consider having seen this work. At what level of ability is this child at? How would you extend these children to help them reach their potential?

A topic on dinosaur's by six year old infants. The teacher asked the children how they could solve the problem of cleaning a dinosaur's teeth. This is Daniel's creative solution.

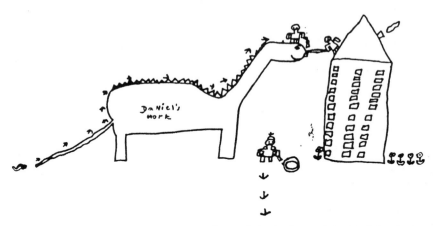

A man climbs the dinosaur's back to its head, where he dangles food in front of its eyes to open its mouth. Another person on the house-roof cleans the dinosaur's teeth with a brush. The person on the ground is putting glue down to keep the dinosaur still. He is wearing a mask because the glue is poisonous.

Daniel

UP IN SPACE.

I am in a space capsule, and I am landing on a big planet with craters in it and it is very cold. I can jump very high and I landed in a crater. There are funny green animals here. There is no one else here except me. I have a space buggy and I drive around space in it. I went on an exploration and found funny flowers with spikes on. They have pink leaves. I was so lonely that I went home.

THE END.

By Karen ........ Age 5½

Notice the skills of writing, the language, knowledge, humour and the human touches at the end.

Elizabeth, aged 12, took a different approach from the rest of her class when they were asked to write an essay on 'conflict'.

Conflict Surprise (a receipt for war)

Ingredients:
5 kg of greed
2 kg of envy
1 raw anger
1 large selfish (very ripe)
5 g of mistrust
7 kg of over ripe violence
3 large misunderstandings (if you have them)

Method:
Using a fist, mix in the greed and envy, let it simmer for an hour. Kick the raw anger in. Squeeze the selfish and add it to thicken the mixture. Sprinkle in the mistrust and stir thoroughly. Using a tank (if you have one) fire in the violence. Beat in the misunderstandings, take a world leader and empty its

mind of peaceful thoughts. Using half the mixture refill the mind. Carefully put the world leader back in its place. Using a sword spread the other half of the mixture across one of the world's countries. Remember to stand back after you have done this; you may become a victim of your own creation. Watch for the after effects, you will enjoy the pain and suffering. You will find it impossible to clean the kitchen when you have finished; all the ingredients will contaminate the rest of the kitchen. Quick tip. For fuller flavour, act first, think later.

In a craft lesson the class were asked to draw a chair from as many angles as possible. Susan, aged 14, whose father is an architect, produced 17 drawings.

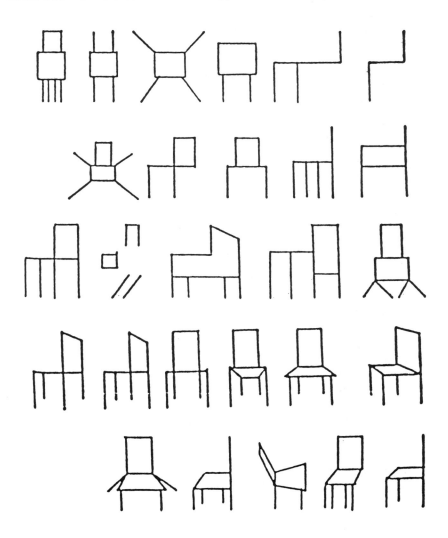

A pen and ink drawing by Imran who was 13 years old. The hand is a most difficult part of the body to draw.

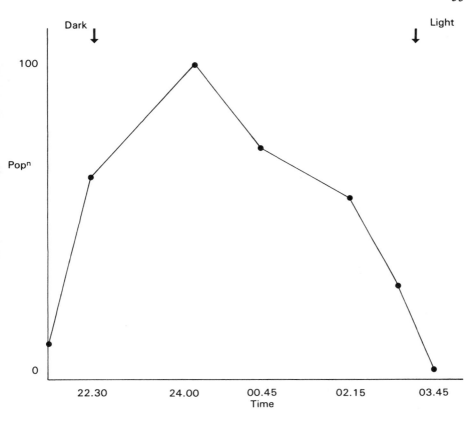

At a Saturday school for gifted children, all of whom had been nominated by their teachers as children who would benefit from being extended, the author did a 2-hour workshop based on woodlice. As a result two 9-year-old boys (David and Sean) stayed up all night counting woodlice on a garden wall. This is their results which proves woodlice are strictly nocturnal.

Of course, parents should know their children better than any teacher possibly can. This is particularly important in the early crucial years when parents will note when children start to talk, to ask questions and start to read. Unfortunately, schools do not ask parents enough about their children before coming to school and later on in their school career. If we believe the concept that parents are the most important teacher a child ever has, then schools really should ask parents to participate more in the enabling curriculum and the following questionnaire should be recommended so that children starting school can be given the appropriate educational experiences at the correct level for that individual child. Their biographical and developmental history summarising the child's early development to identify past obstacles or advantages to learning in the child's health, home, culture circumstances and previous educational history would be most helpful for any teacher. There follows a short questionnaire which should have a covering letter to parents stating that the school is interested in planning appropriate educational experiences for their child and would be grateful for their co-operation. This is followed by a simple questionnaire for children to complete in order to build up a comprehensive profile of the child.

Regretfully, some parents do not know their children well or understand their gifts, talents and precocity; whilst others overestimate their child's abilities. This is where co-operation between school and home is important and will be discussed in Chapter 6.

# PARENT QUESTIONNAIRE

Child's name:...................................................................................................................

Place a tick on the line to indicate how you, honestly, rate the characteristic as listed in your child for his or her age level. (A wide range of possible characteristics is provided, and it would be unrealistic to assume that any one child would be high in all categories.)

| Characteristic | RATING SCALE | | |
| --- | --- | --- | --- |
| | Average | High | Exceptional |
| 1. Concentration (has ability to concentrate, not easily distracted) | | | |
| 2. Knowledge and skills (a wide knowledge of basic skills and factual information, a high level of understanding) | | | |
| 3. Enjoyment of learning | | | |
| 4. Persistence (has ability and desire to stay with a difficult task until it is done, likes competition, not easily distracted) | | | |
| 5. Intellectual curiosity (pursues interests primarily to understand and to satisfy curiosity, questions the ordinary or the unusual, generates questions of his/her own) | | | |
| 6. Acceptance of a challenge (enjoys the challenge of difficult problems, tasks, issues and materials) | | | |
| 7. Perceptiveness (is alert, perceptive and observant beyond his/her years, aware of many stimuli) | | | |

8. Verbal facility (shows marked facility with language, uses words easily and accurately, wide vocabulary)

9. Fluency of ideas (produces a large number of products and ideas, often very quickly)

10. Flexibility (approaches ideas and problems from a number of perspectives, finds alternative ways of solving problems)

11. Originality (often uses original methods of solving problems, can combine ideas and materials in a variety of ways)

12. Reasoning (is logical, often generalises or applies understanding in new situations, expands concepts into broader relationships)

13. Independence in thought (inclined to follow his/her own organisation and ideas rather than the structuring of others)

14. Independence and work habits (requires minimum of adult direction and attention)

15. Independence in action (can plan and organise activities, direct action)

16. Aesthetic appreciation (enjoys and is responsive to beauty in the arts and/or nature)

17. Can produce 'reasons' which may be elaborate for not doing things in the usual way

Please add any other characteristics:

Form completed by:..............................................................................

Date:......................................

# STUDENT QUESTIONNAIRE

Read each statement below. Think carefully about yourself. Write a brief comment by the statement if it sounds like you. Complete the questionnaire as fully as possible. Add anything you wish on the reverse side.

Student's name: ........................................................................................

School: ........................................................................................

---

1. Areas and skills which are easiest in school

---

2. Areas and skills which are hardest in school

---

3. Things enjoyed most

---

4. Things not enjoyed (areas disliked or in which change is desired)

---

5. Areas or activities in which greatest progress is felt

---

6. Preference for working conditions (alone, with others, long periods, where, etc.)

---

7. Sports and games (what activities, evaluation of progress, with whom)

   In school

---

   Out of school

---

8. Use of free time (activities, with whom)

   At school

---

   At home

---

9. Areas in which 'creative' products and freedom of expression are especially enjoyed (writing, music, art, speaking, dance, physical education, drama, construction/manipulative, etc.)

---

10. Hobbies and favourite recreation, collections, can you organise things in unusual ways?

---

11. Lessons out of school – special opportunities

---

12. Television habits:
    Types of programmes preferred

_____

    Frequency of viewing
_____

13. Reading habits:
    Kinds of material preferred

_____

    Amount of time spent reading
_____

14. Special responsibilities or jobs out of school
_____

15. Clubs and organisations (special friends who belong,
    activity leadership role, offices held or desired, etc.)
_____

16. Activities in which family participates as a group
_____

17. Possible vocational choices
_____

18. Educational ambitions
_____

19. I like my work to be perfect
_____

20. Problems encountered
_____

21. I am able to explain things using examples
_____

## Advantages and disadvantages of various methods of identification

| *Method* | *Use and limitations* |
|---|---|
| *Teacher observation/judgement* | Teacher judgement is questionable yet is essential and the trained eyes of the teachers should know their children. But they may miss those who do not conform to accepted standards of work or behaviour, children who present motivational or emotional problems, with belligerent or apathetic attitudes; children who come from homes who do not share the school's ethos and where there are low expectations. |
| *Checklists* | Useful as a quick and easy guide on what to look out for; may not be relevant for individual cases. |
| *General and specific* | Can be misleading, unreliable and lack of validity data. Need time for training teachers, but quick. |

| | |
|---|---|
| *Intelligence tests* | Can be useful as an initial screen to supplement and counterbalance teacher observations, and time efficient. May not identify those with motivational or emotional problems; with reading difficulties or those from different ethnic/cultural backgrounds. |
| *Achievement test batteries* | Helpful in providing more detailed information on a wider range of skills, but subject to some limitations as group tests. Time-consuming for teachers. Will not necessarily identify the true abilities of children nor leadership or social skills. |
| *Creativity tests* | May offer chance to show quality of imagination and divergent thinking in those overlooked by conventional tests above. Difficult to assess, define and measure, and time-consuming to administer. |
| *Individual intelligence tests* | Provide more accurate and reliable information on ability to 'reason' in conventional terms and directly related to identification. May not indicate how a child will perform in class, nor predict achievement in individual cases. Costly in use of time and subject to cultural bias. |
| *Nomination* | Useful information especially from parents to build up a profile. |
| *Renzulli's rating* | Well researched, well constructed and tried but no cut offs given. |
| *Creative learning environments* | The all-important ingredient, encouraging all children to explore their talents; exercise their developing capacity to learn and understand; and to reach the highest potential of which they are capable if they are given the opportunity. |
| *Tests on specific ability* | An attempt to measure difficult constructs such as artistic, unusual or scientific ability. Limited in scope and general lack of information regarding validity. |

# CHAPTER 4

# Provision and Strategies for Teaching

> The education of the child shall be directed to the development of the child's
> personality, talents and mental and physical abilities to their fullest potential.
> (The United Nations Convention on the Rights of the Child (Article 29))

There is no single method of providing for our gifted and talented children
and before we discuss the various models available, it is advisable to
consider the following factors in choosing any one method of provision:

(1)   Does the method chosen properly emphasise the acquisition of a
      higher order of thinking skills and concepts?

(2)   Is the method flexible and open-ended enough for the child to develop
      at its own pace?

(3)   Does the method provide a learning environment as emotionally
      protected as it is intellectually stimulating?

(4)   Is the method chosen likely to alienate a child from its peer group and
      will it be detrimental to the child's subsequent learning, introducing
      factors which will inevitably be repeated later which could
      consequently lead to boredom?

(5)   Does the method chosen provide a process which is more valuable to
      the child, rather than a product which is prestigious to the school?

These are just some of the questions teachers should consider before
adopting any one model.

Davis and Rimm (1989) suggest that a model can provide a useful
theoretical framework within which enriched activities can be planned.
They suggest in their excellent book ten models to range from the
revolving door identification model; Renzulli et al. (1981) give extensive
details regarding the programme philosophy, identification, evaluation and
specific details for carrying out their plan. Other models propose more
general suggestions to the skill and development goals and activities.

Space does not allow a detailed description of these models, but the ten
proposed by Davis and Rimm are as follows:

(1)    The Enrichment Triad Model which lends itself to self-contained classroom adaptation.

This model includes enrichment types 1, 2 and 3, with type 1 giving general exploratory activities, and is intended to expose students to a great many topics. Type 2 is enrichment in group training activities and tries to teach analytical, critical, creative and evaluative thinking, as well as good self concept, values, motivation and both library and research skills.

Type 3 enrichment consists of individual and small group investigations of real problems. The latter type is most appropriate for our most able children.

(2)    The Revolving Door Identification Model (Ranzulli *et al.*, 1981) which is a complete programming guide. They suggest a talent pool which consists of 15–20 per cent of any school population whereby all talent pool students receive type 1 and 2 enrichment, and which students revolve into a resource room to work on projects.

(3)    The Multiple Menu Model, Renzulli (1988) This is a series of five planning guides that suggest sequences and alternatives for teaching content efficiently.

(4)    The Pyramid Project (Cox *et al.*, 1985) is a three-level plan intended to overcome many criticisms of gifted and talented programmes, especially the popular pull-out plan used in the US. This is where above average students are mainstreamed in the normal classroom, more able students are placed in full time special classes and the most able students of all attend magnet or residential schools.

(5)    The Three-Stage Enrichment Model (Feldhusen and Kolloff, 1981) focuses mainly on fostering creative thinking, but also on independent learning skills, research and positive self-concepts. This enrichment programme is developmental in that stage 1 involves short-term teacher-led exercises in creative, critical and logical thinking. Stage 2 involves more complex thinking. Stage 3 activities focus on independent learning by challenging students to define the problem, gather information and creatively report their findings.

(6)    The Guilford and Meeker Structure of Intellect Model (Guilford, 1967, 1977; Meeker and Meeker, 1986) is a rather complex theory of intelligence based upon 120 combinations of 5 operations, 6 products and 4 contents. Meeker uses 26 abilities from the Guilford Model to guide and diagnose specific learning abilities, especially those related to creativity, mathematics, reading and writing. This approach can be useful in identifying a gifted minority and disadvantaged students.

(7)    This is a four-stage model (Treffinger, 1975) to increase self-directedness, the four stages being, the command style which is teacher-directed; the task style in which students select from teacher-prepared activities; the peer-partner style which enables students to

make more decisions about learning goals and activities and fourthly, the self-directed style whereby a student creates the choices, makes the selections and chooses the amount of working time.

(8)    The Autonomous Learner Model (Betts, 1985) fits 'usage within the classroom' and is a recently completed programming guide which includes the five dimensions of orientating students and others to giftedness and to the content and purposes of the programme. This also involves individual development in areas of learning skills, personal understanding, inter-personal skills, student enrichment activities, as well as career development.

(9)    The Williams Model (1970) for developing thinking and feeling processes explains how his eighteen teaching strategies may be classified according to the three categories of the enrichment triad model.

(10)   The Taylor Multiple Talent Totem Pole Model (1978) states that learning activities focus upon developing academic ability, creativity, communicating, predicting, organising and decision making and evaluation.

The reader is referred to these models, which may be helpful in making a decision as to what programme to propose for any group of students in any single school. For the purposes of this book, it is proposed to investigate further the six categories that Ogilvie (1973) proposed as talent areas for these children, which in turn is very similar to the US Office of Education Statement which was the model used in Chapter 3 on identification. The thoughtful teacher will consider all of these models, along with more specific strategies which will be discussed later, such as enrichment.

## Individual studies

This allows the curriculum to develop out of students' own interests and obviously children are more motivated to do better on a topic if it comes from their own interests. This also enables them to take ownership for their own learning, to do good research and the whole process begins with the ability to use the library well. Whichever way this is undertaken, teachers have a responsibility to see that the students understand the basic steps in preparing their research and topic report, which includes choosing the subject, planning, outlining, gathering information from a variety of sources, writing, revising and preparing the final report. Another factor is the opportunity for students to work with people who have a like enthusiasm and knowledge related to the student's choice of subject. This also means that a teacher has to be humble enough to ask an expert, either in the school, to mentor a student, or to ask for support from outside experts in the community. This should be encouraged, because we have to realise that with the speed and growth of knowledge, no teacher can possibly know all there is to know about any one subject, and some of these outstanding children need the stimulus, maybe only acquired from someone with the depth of knowledge that an average teacher cannot possibly have.

Let us now consider the six areas in our definition and see how these can be provided and encouraged in our more able children.

## Creativity

One of the goals of gifted education is to develop creative and imaginative thinking, as well as problem solving. An important aim here is for gifted students to be encouraged to function as creative and productive people in their society. This encouragement comes from the provision of appropriate learning environments and learning experiences, and are designed for the production of ideas that reflect growth from the known to the original.

Recommendations for creative teaching include teacher enthusiasm, encouraging self-initiated projects, acceptance of individual differences in our children, the encouragement of divergent thinking and certainly looking beyond IQ scores. Creative learning can result in children achieving higher, improved motivation, self-confidence and a better attitude towards school. The learning experiences should be designed to provide for the development of creativity through the integration of cognitive skills, affective skills, intuition and talents in a specific area.

Although there is still some difficulty in defining the concept of creativity, many researchers have tried to make the term more tangible by identifying specific creative abilities; Guilford (1967), Torrance (1966), Davis and Rimm (1989), and the most widely quoted four are:

Fluency – quantity; the ability to generate many solutions or alternatives. For example:

> Think of several possible ways to –
> Come up with ideas for –
> List as many ways to –

Flexibility – thinking in a variety of categories and taking several approaches. For example:

> Think of different kinds of reasons for –
> List as many different ways to –
> What are the different kinds of –

Originality – this is the ability to arrive at novel, unusual, non-conforming conclusions – uniqueness. For example:

> Think of unique and unusual ways to –
> Think of ideas no-one else will think of –

Elaboration – the ability to add details and develop ideas. For example:

> Think of details to develop your main idea –
> Add supplementary ideas to make the basic idea clearer –

These creative abilities are very much encouraged in future problem solving activities and the odyssey of the mind programmes in the US, and are aimed at promoting creative thinking and problem solving. These units of instruction, such as the study of inventions and inventing themselves, excite and challenge gifted students, while tapping into the innovative spirit they possess.

*Creative activities* (some suggested activities used by the author over the years)

Living on a sand-dune
In science, one of the areas of interest for these children is what does it mean to be alive? After some initial discussion about the life processes and the characteristics of all living things, the children will soon realise that these life processes are carried out in many diverse ways. This activity enables the children to design their own organism, remembering that life on a sand-dune is a tough environment in which to survive.

Activity
(1)   Create an organism that can survive and perform all life functions on a dry, windblown and mobile sand-dune.
(2)   Your three-dimensional organism can be made of any materials using common household items.
(3)   You will be asked to present your organism to the class, and justify its design one week from today.

Evaluation
Based on how well the life functions can be carried out, remembering limiting properties of the organism's environment.

*A tall structure* (science, maths, design technology)

Overview
At times, students should be encouraged to practise generating the ideas beyond the norm. They need the opportunity to approach a problem in a new way. This activity gives them the chance to do just that. It can be used by challenging problem solving activity.

Activity
(1)   Work in groups of two or three and design and build the tallest free-standing structure using houshold and basic classroom materials available.
(2)   Each group should be given one sheet of paper, some sellotape and scissors.

Remembering the sequence of steps discussed earlier, it would be a good idea for the small groups of children to discuss their plan of action before construction commences. This is a good activity for teaching co-operation in groups.

Creative activity appears often to be simply a special problem solving activity characterised by novelty. Here are just a few suggestions:

(1) If you were king of the castle, what would you do if your serfs went on strike?

(2) List all the qualities you look for in a friend. Which is the most important? Why?

(3) List all the reasons you can think of for eating vegetables.

(4) Think of several colloquial expressions, for example a hole in one, or down in the mouth, or a pain in the neck. Illustrate, and elaborate on each expression.

(5) Pretend you are a fashion designer and predict what the new fashion will be in the year 2000. Think of as many original fads as you can and pick out your favourite.

Creativity is the ability to see, to be aware and to respond. Here are some examples:

(1) You are probably aware that the rings in a tree tunk help determine the age of the tree. The tree trunk however, also twists axially as it grows. Brainstorm to find reasons why this may occur, and also what phenomena it might help us to understand.

(2) Create a sound map of your school.

(3) Mrs Jones has been left 46 cats in her aunt's will. She is at a loss as to what to do with these felines, yet she will lose £100,000 if she gives the cats away without checking each potential owner out most thoroughly. List as many ways as possible as to what to do with all these cats.

Originality is simply a fresh pair of eyes. Here are some examples to encourage this:

(1) Write a poem that describes your personality and includes your name.

(2) Describe what a television set sees as it sits and watches you.

(3) With the invention of CDs, records have become somewhat obsolete. Name all the things you could do with your out-dated record collection.

(4) Think of as many reasons as you can for re-cycling waste material from your home and school, and list how they could be re-used.

(5) List 25 ways to keep you from being bored in school, at home or on a long car journey.

(6) Five new planets have just been discovered. Think of different names for these planets and give reasons for why you have chosen the names.

(7)    A teacher or parent could collect unusual headlines from newspapers
or magazines, or better still, encourage the children to bring them to
school. The more unusual or potentially humorous the headline, the
better.

Children are then randomly assigned a different headline and asked
to write a brief new article on what they think the headline is about.
The children should be encouraged to use fluency, flexibility and
originality in coming up with their ideas, as well as elaboration in
fleshing out the story.

## Creative questions

Teachers and parents can use the art of questioning creatively in the
classroom and at home. Creative questioning, skilfully employed, causes
students to develop both their sense of wonder and their communication
skills, though they should always have plenty of time to think of
imaginative responses. Such questions could be as follows:

(1)    How many uses can you think of for a . . . .?
(2)    What would happen if there were no . . . .?
(3)    What could you do to improve a . . . .?
(4)    How might you feel if you were a . . . .?

Ask children to make creative choices through use of the following
questions and ask them to say why:

(1)    Would you rather be the wind or a river?
(2)    Would you rather be a bird or a cat?
(3)    Would you rather be the Prime Minister or a Liverpool football
player?

The creative process is any thinking process which solves a problem in an
original and useful way.

## Leadership

In our definition, any field of human endeavour is represented by its leaders,
including the creative arts, technology, research, exploration, leading a
business or church or sports team. Definitions of leadership usually amount
to a list of characteristics and skills of leaders, and these include, as we have
noted earlier, confidence, being well regarded, adaptability, high
responsibility, skills in communication, planning, group dynamics and
public relations, amongst others. Plowman (1981) includes six aspects of
leadership which are, being charismatic, intuitive, creative, evaluative,
analytical and synergistic. These, and others, can be used as objectives for
creating a leadership curriculum.

Leadership education can include teaching the students about leadership styles by looking at biographies of great leaders; teaching students the skills of leadership, putting students into a leadership role, as well as teaching them the skills of communication, planning, problem solving and decision making. Magoon (1981) described five leadership activities: mentorship, in-school leadership projects, community projects, simulations and classrooms monitors. All this involves the teacher in providing the opportunity by having a creative learning environment which was discussed earlier.

## *What makes a leader?* (suggested exercises)

The following leadership portraits may help children to consider how leaders differ from each other and how some characteristics may be common to them all. An attempt to produce a profile of leadership characteristics, listing such qualities as bravery, integrity and charisma, can be the basis of a profitable discussion, although it may not be easy to agree what these things mean. In discussing leadership,, a number of questions might be asked, including:

(1) Do leaders lead every group they join?
(2) Are leaders more interested in themselves than others?
(3) Is it possible for a loner to be a leader?
(4) Are leaders created by situations?
(5) Are leaders achievers or exponents of excellence?
(6) Do leaders operate through fear?
(7) Do groups accept leaders because they help to get what the group wants?
(8) Do leaders really persuade groups that they want what the leader wants?

It may be helpful to arrange this list of leadership roles in order of priority and add other roles to it.

## *Bob Geldof*

Bob Geldof was born in 1954 in Dublin. His mother died when he was very young. After a number of casual jobs he went to Canada as a pop music journalist. Returning to Dublin in 1979 he and some friends formed the highly successful Boomtown Rats pop group.

When he saw newsfilm of starving Ethiopians in 1984, he was so moved that he decided he must do something to raise money to help these people. He persuaded over fifty musicians, record producers and others to make a single *Do They Know its Chrismas?* It sold 3 million copies in Britain alone and raised £8 million worldwide for Ethiopia. He then had the idea of 'The Global Jukebox'. The 'Live Aid' concert which followed created sixteen hours of live entertainment that reached 80 per cent of the world's TV sets and raised over £50 million.

Bob is continuing with other campaigns. 'It is important to make a grand gesture, so that you can focus the attention of governments. We have kept millions of people alive. Now we must give them life... this means more money for long-term projects.'

- What particular leadership qualities do you think Bob Geldof possesses?
- Do you think it accurate to describe him as a 'media hero'?
- In what ways do you think that being a pop star helped Bob Geldof to influence people?
- What do you think people will remember about Bob Geldof in fifty years time?

*Martin Luther King*

Martin Luther King was born in 1929 in the American South, living against a background of poverty, racial discrimination and the terror of the Ku Klux Klan. As a young Baptist minister in Alabama he became involved in the Civil Rights movement. Only eight years later he led a great Civil Rights march to Washington with over 200,000 people, black and white, taking part. It was in his speech at the Lincoln Memorial that he challenged America with his famous declaration: 'I have a dream that one day this nation will rise up, live out the true meaning of its creed... that all men are equal.'

In the same year, King was awarded the Nobel Peace Prize of £10,000. He gave it all to the cause of Civil Rights.

Throughout his life he preached against violence of all kinds. He opposed America's part in the Vietnam War. His work was bitterly attacked in many parts of the US. Civil Rights workers, black and white, were beaten or murdered. 'Every man should have something to die for. A man who won't die for something isn't fit to live.'

At aged 38, on a motel balcony in Memphis, Tennessee, Martin Luther King was shot dead by white extremist James Earl Ray.

- What part do you think that race and place of birth played in making Martin Luther King a leader?
- Do you think that being a church minister helped or hindered his campaign?
- King was a great orator. How important is oratory to leadership?
- What do you think kept him going in times of hardship and danger?

*Florence Nightingale*

While travelling abroad, Florence Nightingale's parents christened her after the Italian city where she was born. As she grew up, they thought she was a quiet child who worried and brooded too much. They were not pleased when she announced that she wanted to take up the poorly regarded task of nursing the sick. Nevertheless, at the age of twenty-four, she began a ten year study of nursing practices in England and Europe, becoming convinced that there was a need for women with a sense of vocation to take up the work. Her first job was the little sought one of matron in a mental hospital.

In 1854, when she heard about the terrible conditions of the wounded British soldiers in the Crimean War, she offered to lead a party of women nurses to work in the Military Hospital at Scutari. There she found conditions were appalling. The wounded, lying in disease-ridden squalor, died of fever rather than their wounds. She was ruthless in the use of her links with influential people, completely overhauling the Army medical services and reducing the hospital deathrate by over 40 per cent. Soldiers blessed the 'lady with the lamp' who overcame resistance from officials to obtain the supplies and improvements that she saw were needed.

Returning to London amid public acclaim in 1856, she set up the Nightingale Training School for Nurses at St Thomas's Hospital. Using money collected by public subscription, she raised the status of nursing and created a new kind of nurse who took the 'Nightingale' method all over the world.

- What obstacles did Florence Nightingale have to overcome?
- What qualities of leadership did she show?
- How similar was her life to that of other upper class women of her time?
- Do you think you would have been able to work under her leadership?
- Are there any causes today that need a new 'Florence Nightingale'?

*Mother Teresa*

In 1910 a little girl called Agnes was born in Yugoslavia. By the time she was twelve, her Christian upbringing led her to feel that God had a particular purpose for her. Her wish to join the Loretto Order of Nuns who taught in Calcutta was fulfilled when she was sent to the Loretto Abbey in Dublin in 1928. As Sister Teresa, she taught geography at St Mary's High School in Calcutta. Every day she saw poor and sick people who lived, slept and died in the streets in conditions that were often worse than those provided for animals. She decided that in order to help these people she had to live amongst them.

In 1946, she was granted permission by the Pope to live outside the Convent with the slum people of Calcutta and was trained as a nurse by the

American Missionary Sisters. By 1950, Mother Teresa and her helpers (among whom were doctors and nurses) had formed the Missionaries of Charity. Food and money were sent to Centres all over the world for the relief of the sick and for the care of poor, unwanted and abandoned children. At her request, a new group, the Missionary Brothers of Charity, was formed. They opened homes for the physically and mentally handicapped, as well as schools, youth centres and health clinics. An international appeal spread the work across the world.

In 1979, Mother Teresa was awarded the Nobel Peace Prize. Today, she still travels the world encouraging her co-workers, but she always returns to the slums of Calcutta.

- Some people seem to have the ability to attract the help of others. Why do you think this is so?
- Not everyone can devote all their energies to a single purpose. Can you think of others who have?
- Where do you think Mother Teresa found the strength for her work?

## Leadership

A leader: 1. recognises a need; 2. achieves a goal; 3. takes action; 4. takes responsibility; 5. provides expertise; 6. sets an example; 7. encourages the less able; 8. pools and focuses ideas; 9. controls and unifies; 10. plans; 11. creates policy.

Having looked at biographies of great leaders and having listed their characteristics, it would be an idea to extend this activity by then looking at power structures or spheres of influence operating in any classroom or youth group to find out who are the most influential members of the class or group, and when is their influence greatest?

## The nature of leadership

| Leadership | vs. | Management |
|---|---|---|
| Pull | | Push |
| Empower | | Control |
| Long-term vision | | Short-term goals |
| Group intelligence | | Single intelligence |
| Using group skills | | Own skills |
| Respect and trust | | Patronise |
| High performance workgroup | | Rigid hierarchy |
| Bottom–up | | Top–down |
| Qualitative measures | | Quantitative measures |

Reprinted with permission from digital Equipment Corporation (1991).

*Projects for potential leaders*

In everyday life people may be thrown into situations that call for leadership, in which they must think ahead, establish priorities, make decisions, keep their nerve, persuade others to follow a course of action. There are absolutely no right answers in a situation like this, but some actions may be better than others.

Rescue

You and two friends are on the way to school. You are surprised to find letters blowing about the pavement from an open post office pillar box. Not far away, just around the corner, besides his van, lies the postman. He is not moving. What would be the first thing you would tell your friends to do? What would you do? What would you not do? Make a list of actions in order that should be taken.

Good cause

Your neighbour's two year old daughter needs special surgery to cure a rare disease. Funds are needed to send her and her mother abroad to the only hospital which is able to help. What could you do to help raise funds? Can you think of a service or goods for which people might be willing to pay? How could you persuade other people to help you? How could you organise a fundraising project? Who might help you with advice on running your fundraising effort? Draw up a timetable for the project. Make an estimate of the costs of running such a project.

Mount an emergency

Leading a lightweight camping holiday of six people in the Alps, you have all the supplies needed for a week's stay in the mountains. Although it is a summer holiday, the weather has become unsettled with hail and thunderstorms at this height. You have previously left a note of your intended route with a mountain rescue organisation.

On the second night out and six miles from the nearest village you awake to find that John, a member of the party, has rolled out of his tent and fallen from a small ridge. He has injured his ankle and has a nasty bump on his head. Another member of the party suggests that it is John's own fault for pitching his tent in a stupid place. Consider the immediate and long-term problems. Decide together with other members of your camping party which course of action you should take and in what order things should be done. Which of the characteristics of the members of your camping party would be useful in this situation?

*Leadership discussion points*

Here are some recipes for success. Do you agree with the opinion expressed?

Many business leaders have offered their views on the secrets of their success, but they have not always agreed:

> 'Life is based on seeing, listening and experimenting, but experimenting is the most important.'
> (Soichiro Honda)

> 'How did I make my fortune? By always selling too soon. Sell, regret and grow rich.'
> (Nathan Rothschild)

> 'Don't be conformist. A businessman who wants to be successful cannot afford to imitate others. He must be original, imaginative, resourceful and be an entirely self-reliant entrepreneur.'
> (John Paul Getty)

> 'When you want something from a person, think of what you can give him in return. Let him think it is he who is coming off best.' (Ernest Oppenheimer)

## Psychomotor ability

The nature of psychomotor ability, as well as the whole structure of physical education and sport in this country is very complex. The development of physical skills to full potential involves a successful interaction between genetic and environmental factors. A knowledge of the former informs our understanding, whilst an appreciation of the latter ensures that we become enablers. Environmental factors are, therefore, the most significant in the promotion of excellence. There is a need for a collaborative strategy between physical education and sport, and physical recreation and health for the development of physical skills to the full potential of the whole person. Physical activity is part of our heritage and psychomotor competence can only enhance the quality of all our lives, as well as allowing us to marvel at the achievements of the gifted athlete. If we believe in a healthy mind and a healthy body, then we need to have a broad view of physical education and sport integrated with other aspects.

Firstly, we need a procedural knowledge – knowing how in the areas of athletics, dance, games (running games, over the net games, striking games, creating games) and swimming, but it is more than giving enrichment in these different games, because there is knowing that part of the subject and this includes: 1. codes of conduct; 2. health education; 3. first aid; 4. information about after-school activities; 5. decision making; 6. tactics and strategy; 7. criticism and analysis; 8. rules necessary for safety and hygiene; 9. laws of the sport or game; 10. a knowledge of moral, social, aesthetic values gained through physical education and sport.

## Concepts

1. Awareness of space; 2. understanding of effort, such as weight and time, technique, themes, form, principles of play, and adaptability.

*Attitudes*

Some of the attitudes that make for a whole person who really reaches their full potential in the area of psychomotor ability are: 1. co-operation; 2. courage; 3. consideration; 4. enthusiasm; 5. determination; 6. initiative; 7. social ability; 8. sportsmanship; 9. self-motivation; 10. supportive and a sense of humour.

*Skills*

There are numerous skills to be taught and enhanced amongst these children in order to reach their potential which includes: 1. gymnastics; 2. balance skills; 3. weight transference skills; 4. shape skills; 5. flight; 6. tactical skills; 7. team skills, as well as movement skills and body awareness.

It is obvious from the foregoing that this idealistic scheme is very demanding on time and necessitates well-trained specialist teachers, and because of the pressure on the timetable for both content and time, it is suggested that the introduction of sports and dance clinics or teach-ins during and outside the school day would be necessary. Home coaching packages could be drawn up and directed by the school, but supported by parents. A continental style day with academic time during the morning and compulsory physical education in the afternoon is to be commended. This should allow for collaboration with those outside agencies which can assist with facilities and coaching expertise.

Ideally, every child should have physical education every day and a progressive system for the development of gymnastic skills, for example, from the pre-school years through to Olympic standard should be available.

Teachers should be made aware of the competitive structures available through inter-club, inter-county, regional zone, national and international levels. This structure takes account of relative excellence in competitive gymnastics, for example, as well as giving individual direct access to the top of the tree. This may be an almost impossible task within any one school, but we have to be humble enough to admit we cannot do everything and make use of the considerable resources available, including that of retired performers; teachers and parents should be encouraged to continue in sport, in coaching and in administration. This will enable our talented children to have increased participation and the specialisation to cater for giftedness in any given area of psychomotor ability. A school system, of course, is concerned with the total development of the child and this must include enhancing the considerable psychomotor ability that some children have and the availability of sport for all.

Earlier in this book, it was stated that it would be grounded in the reality of the classroom. It is essential to have a thorough knowledge base for this work, but the following is an example of some of the difficulties in catering adequately for these children.

There are no 'hard and fast rules' to different types of grouping in PE. It is quite possible that a low ability group could be keener/better motivated in PE, than a group with higher academic ability. What tends to happen though, is the brighter group are easier to teach/control as they take information in and are able to act on that information. In general their behaviour/span of concentration/social skills are better than the less able students. Safety is of paramount importance, therefore discipline has to be good. The following is a comprehensive school Head of PE Department writing about some of the difficulties of ability grouping.

> When the whole year group are on together they are divided into equal numbers, done mainly by tutor groupings (as this is the most convenient method). Certain individuals may be kept apart.
> Year 7 and Year 11 have some mixed (boys/girls) lessons. We hope to carry this into Year 8 in September 1991.
> A few years ago we did try to group into ability: 'A' - the athletic/skilful students; 'B' - the average/well-motivated; 'C' - the poor attenders, badly behaved, less able. This did not work very well as the 'A' group were too arrogant and tended to think they knew it all. The 'C' group numbers were erratic and the ability so poor that progress was difficult. The best group being 'B' - a pleasure to teach.
> This academic year we have also had to modify the curriculum, in particular Year 9 girls. They are not interested in 'skill exercises' and in order to get them to bring kit on a regular basis, a more flexible approach is required.

Hopefully, earlier suggestions in this section will help considerably. There is, however, another side of physical education that is the integration of minds with physical bodies. In the past, schools have required the development of the physical body as a separate entity. There is a need to understand energy balance and the problems of stress, to name just two areas. There are many forms of relaxation that can be used to develop the skill of physically reducing tension. Another area which should be taught these children through PE is sensory awareness, which is important in expanding the abilities of people. Young children particularly make sense of their environment by using their senses, which includes visual, tactile, auditory and awareness. See Clarke (1983) for further information.

When we discuss intelligence, it is important that we do not just think of school activities as the more we understand the human brain, the more we come to realise that it includes our emotional health, our physical ability and health, our creative and intuitive selves along with our visual and verbal thinking.

## Academic ability

Much encouragement is given to our children in schools regarding their cognitive development and often to the detriment of the other talent areas we are discussing in this chapter. It is generally acknowledged that far too much classroom learning is concerned with traditional academic knowledge and routine skills, than teaching children to think, to reason and to solve problems in a creative way. David and Rimm (1989) suggest there are three basic ways to teach thinking:

(1) Strengthening the intellectual abilities and skills through practice and exercise.
(2) Helping students learn conscious and deliberate strategies for reasoning, problem solving and critical thinking.
(3) Increasing students' understanding of their own and others' thinking.

All these involve inductive reasoning, which is used whenever the thinker reaches a conclusion which is somewhat supported, and deductive reasoning, which is a process whereby the thinker reaches a conclusion which is necessitated by the premises. There is still some debate when a person is using deductive reasoning or using inductive reasoning. Some philosophers answer this query by saying that the thinker is using whatever kind of reasoning he thinks he is using. Recently Herrmann (1987) speaking at the World Conference on gifted and talented children in Sydney explained research which has found that some kinds of thinking primarily involve the left hemisphere of the brain, some kinds that primarily involve the right hemisphere, whereas other kinds of thinking involve both hemispheres and particularly utilising the corpus callosum which connects the two hemispheres.

It appears to me that most kinds of subjects taught in school involve primarily the left hemisphere, and when you look at the British National Curriculum, it appears that it is heavily biased this way. If this is proved to be correct, then we are giving children an unbalanced curriculum. For example, pure deductive reasoning, spelling, reading and arithmetic calculations are all left brain. But such things as recognition of patterns, the ability to generalise and consequently at least some kinds of inductive reasoning, appear to involve primarily the right hemisphere. Taking this to its logical conclusion, this means that English, mathematics and science, which are the three core subjects taking most of the time available, are largely left hemisphere subjects, whereas the creative arts, which include perception, fantasy and enjoyment, as well as the ability to see the broad picture, originates in the right hemisphere. Since education then seems to concentrate on left hemisphere thinking activities, and since it is the right hemisphere which is needed for seeing patterns and making generalisations, this could well be the reason why students seldom automatically transfer learning, even within the same subject area, let alone from one subject area to another, or to everyday life situations. For example, relating what the child has done in the science laboratory to solving problems in our world. It also appears that either the right hemisphere or the corpus callosum is used a great deal in drawing reasonable inferences, recognising cause and effect, reasoning by analogy, spatial perception, recognising relations, creativity and asking and answering such questions as 'what would happen if'? Much of this side of the right brain which is the inductive thinking side can be taught and encouraged in these children.

As academic superiority is perhaps the major reason still why gifted and talented children are initially identified, then such skills as these should be recognised and encouraged. Of course, it is not just a matter of how well a child is performing in academic subjects, but a child's study skills approach to a problem and application. For example Bloom (1985) found that many students engaged in detailed individual activities for long periods of time, asked many questions, learned through observation, enjoyed reading and experimentation, made use of the knowledge gained. However, this is not always the case. A child may be intellectually superior, but poor on the application. Gifted is as gifted does. Some of these children can be described as gifted underachievers, and these children often need a great deal of support and counselling, which will be discussed later.

Thinking skills can be strengthened and improved through exercises in a similar way as a sports person practises. Creative thinking may be taught directly by helping students to understand creative people and creative processes. Critical thinking may be taught by teaching children to observe and look critically at opinion or a newspaper article. Examples of Bloom's taxonomy have already been discussed and much of the work of teaching thinking skills has recognised his impact on this area. His taxonomy describes progressively higher levels of cognitive activity.

At the knowledge and comprehensive stage, students deal with definitions, facts and categories, as well as relationships and theories. While this is necessary for all students, often gifted and talented students who have a strong knowledge base can move higher up taxonomy and apply rules and principles, analyse, hypothesise, synthesise and evaluate the accuracy, value and efficiency of an idea or a course of action.

Children should also be encouraged in the teaching of thinking. This area, commonly called a metacognition, is thinking about thinking, and students should understand their thinking strategies, understand why and when and how these strategies may be used. The de Bono (1973) Cort programmes are prototypes of metacognition and children are encouraged to function better, not only to be more proficient at solving problems, but enjoying thinking. The Cort thinking skills are taught in a direct metacognitive fashion, whereby children consciously understand the value of each skill and when, why and how it should be applied. There are some 50 Cort thinking skills and these are just some examples:

(1) Challenging existing ways of doing things as a means of stimulating new ideas.

(2) Solving problems by thinking about problem requirements.

(3) Directing something according to their needs and requirements.

(4) Decision making, which requires considering the factors involved, objectives, priorities, consequences and possible alternatives.

(5) Recognising contradictory information which can lead to false conclusions.

The following are a few examples of this type of thinking exercise which teachers and parents should consider teaching their children:

(1) Suppose you were born 100 years from now, how would your life be different from what it is now?

(2) Scientists are gradually finding more cures for different types of cancer. However, it seems that cancer is still killing many more people than it did, say 50 years ago. Why do you suppose this is so?

(3) If you could run your school any way you wanted to, what would you do? Who would you have to teach in it and who would attend your school? Would you have any rules regarding how students should behave in your school? Would you have any rules about school uniform? What would you do about someone who did not obey the rules? Who would pay for the cost of running the school? Would you allow anyone from any age group to attend?

(4) Mary has a blind friend who doesn't know what an elephant is. The friend has heard of an elephant and knows it is an animal, but that is all the friend knows about elephants. How should Mary go about describing an elephant to her friend?

(5) In many parts of the world there are many deaths caused by traffic accidents. It has been estimated that over 50 per cent of fatal accidents involve drivers who have been drinking alcohol. What do you think should be done to reduce the number of fatal accidents?

(6) What would you do if a real UFO landed on the school playing field not far from where you were standing?

(7) On arriving home from school one day, you walked into the kitchen and put the light switch on, but nothing happens. The light does not go on, the light bulb does not flash. What would you do?

**Providing for gifted and talented children – a summary**

*Considerations*

What do we want gifted and talented students to be or do as an outcome of their education?

Is the purpose of education for the gifted and talented to promote the development of self or the contributions they can make to society?

Is learning how to learn more important than what is being learned?

Is quantity or quality the focus of a programme?

Should learning emphasise the assimilation of information or the development of thinking processes?

Is the progress of the gifted and talented measured against the group, the average or the self?

Is the winning of prizes, and 'A's' an indicator of school success?

## Implications

The answers to these questions reflect personal biases, experiences and knowledge. Reviewing the purposes for a gifted and talented programme and understanding the elements of a programme can shape values for the programme. What is to be valued for the gifted and talented cannot be separated from research data about the characteristics and needs of these students, the contemporary feelings of society about education, and the interests, background and attitudes of the students.

What INSET is required to increase staff awareness of the need of these children across the curriculum?

Providing a balanced and challenging curriculum which is flexible enough to take account of all children.

## Application

The aim and objectives of an educational programme for the gifted and talented should stress the development of the self as the top priority. Objectives which are open-ended allow for student determination in the learning process. Aims and objectives which are student written are consonant with the concept of self-direction. Goals and objectives which stress the attainment of learning skills such as research, inquiry and problem solving are conducive to teaching students how to learn.

Keeping and monitoring of children's records and profile is essential.

Making sure that these children have some power over their own curriculum which is their entitlement.

## Teachers of the gifted

A great teacher never strives to explain his vision – he simply invites you to stand beside him and see for yourself.          (Rev R. Inman)

The teacher has the unique opportunity to make provision for the potentially gifted child to develop and mature and that child can eventually become a positive and valued member of the society which needs him. Children, however, also have the right to develop fully as individuals, and it is the right of every child to be child-like. The sympathetic, perceptive, empathising teacher should be aware of some children's lack of synchronisation with their peers, possibly their family and their time.

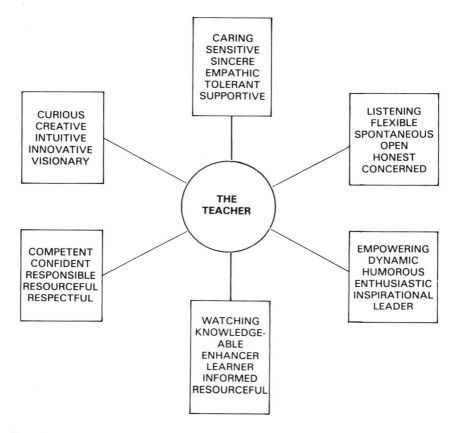

**Figure 4.1**

Teachers should understand the feelings of frustration and isolation which can be present when intellectual development surges ahead of the emotional and physical. He will be conscious of the possible disparity between intellectual and social needs; the needs of advanced intellectual development compared with the basic human needs of security and social acceptance.

Such teachers need to be sufficiently mature themselves and capable of accepting children with their high abilities. In addition, teachers need to be humble, accepting of the role of being a learner with the child. Gallagher (1985) identifies three needs of paramount importance; firstly, the need to help these children develop study skills; secondly the need to encourage bright pupils to develop skills of higher level thinking, and thirdly, the need to be rewarded for scholastic achievement, whilst at the same time retaining an identity with the class group. Here, you will note, the emphasis is on the cognitive development of children, whereas we must remember our broader definition and cater for the talent areas that many children have.

Maker (1982b) requires that teachers have a good knowledge of their subjects:

(1) Sympathetic understanding of child development
(2) Confidence
(3) Skill in developing flexible and interesting material
(4) Highly developed skills of questioning and explaining
(5) Willingness to guide rather than dictate, allowing pupils to develop independence of mind and action
(6) Proven success as a teacher in the regular classroom
(7) An ability to make mistakes

Undoubtedly one could argue that all children would benefit from contact with teachers possessing these qualities. Both teachers, and especially head teachers, need the necessary qualities of leadership as one of the talent areas that some children have.

It often surprises me that we do not ask children nearly often enough what they would like to learn, what their ideal classroom would be like, how they could solve some of the problems of the school, and to give examples. Endean and George (1982) asked 9–10 year old gifted children what they thought the ideal teacher should be like and the following list is quite a challenge to any teacher.

*The ideal science teacher*

Almost all required that the teacher be master of his subject. Some (girls) specified that the teacher was to be well educated in all areas, not just in science. Almost as universally prescribed was a sense of humour. It was felt this was conducive to an easy but not slack atmosphere in the classroom, and it was mentioned that it helped to make the lesson fun, and so helped to motivate them to learn. The paragon is also required to be a good communicator. He must be able to convey the essence of difficult new concepts in a readily understood and simple manner. The importance of his using 'everyday language' and being able to give 'everyday examples' was stressed. One respondent added that if there were not an everyday application to hand, then the teacher should be able to supply a good analogy.

A group of respondents (girls) placed considerable emphasis on the teacher explaining individual errors to students, so that they could understand their own mistakes, and avoid making the same errors in future. Several (mainly boys) prescribed a teacher who felt personally involved with the pupils and with the work they produced. An equally sized group (mainly girls) stressed the importance of the teacher being able to inspire zest and having the power to motivate them to learn.

Generally, the ideal teacher should set up and maintain a well-structured but informal learning environment within which pupils could suggest their own ideas and experiments (this from the girls), discuss ideas and errors, and, due to his consummate pedagogical skills, all could progress at their own individual rate without holdups.

On another occasion the author asked a group of nine year old children at a summer school what they expected from a teacher: discipline; sense of humour; caring; sympathy when in difficulty; ability to explain problems; encouragement to look forward to lessons; no favourites; good appearance; variety in lessons; learning made easy!; understanding of pupils' viewpoint.

Some researchers would have taken considerable time to come up with this list!

Perhaps we should therefore, ask ourselves the following questions in the light of the above:

(1)   What am I doing to encourage and develop interest that is shown by individual children?

(2)   How far are the children learning independently?

(3)   What attitudes are the more able children developing towards their own ability, and am I acting as a positive counsellor and enhancer?

(4)   Are the children positively involved by their attitudes towards their less able peers?

(5)   What opportunity do these children have to work with a group of like-minded and similar ability children?

Head teachers can make things happen in their school, they are responsible for school policy, whether it be for special needs children, the needs of our multi-cultural society, equal opportunities, the new technologies, the home and environment, or the children we are discussing here. It is because of the power of head teachers in our school system that we pause and consider what are the necessary qualities of leadership we should expect from head teachers and the fact that they are not just managers of resources. Good head teachers stand out by being different, they question assumptions and are suspicious of traditions. They make decisions based on fact and not on prejudice and have a preference for innovation. Such leaders are observant and sensitive to people, they know their team well, they have a talented pool of staff and develop mutual confidence within their team.

Head teachers should state clear objectives and encourage a sense of security by defining territory for individual action. They should delegate real authority and should not interfere unless it is necessary, and they should praise more often than they criticise. Maslow's (1968) hierarchy of human needs is for all mankind, not just for gifted and talented children, as we shall discuss in Chapter 6. If we can select and educate head teachers with these characteristics, then our teachers who have an exhausting job to do will follow them with respect and even with affection and a sense of curiosity, because they make life enjoyable for the team by the promise of surprise, excitement, but above all, solid achievement for all our children. If good teachers then are the most valuable resource in creating opportunities for our gifted and talented children, time is the second most valuable. Of course, teachers and time are both costly. There is no escaping the fact that it takes time to maintain a highly-trained professional teaching force, and as we believe that children are the most natural precious resource that we possess, then both time and money should be found for them.

*Courses for teachers*

In initial teacher training, quite frankly it is felt there is insufficient time to do justice to the many areas that students today need to cover in order to be confident and competent teachers in the classroom. There are obviously competing pressures coupled with the varying concerns of staff, and it is not easy to make a case for a substantial part of any teacher training course in the area of gifted education. It is probably best left to near the end of a Bachelor of Education degree course when students can capitalise upon the wealth of knowledge, skills and experience acquired earlier in the course. In initial teacher training, students should be trained to be made aware of our most able children, to understand the needs of all children and how they should be educated as whole people. It is appropriate to deal with the issue in the general context of catering for individual differences, rather than as a totally separate issue. Thus, general matters arising in connection with child development, learning strategies and individual differences have to be considered first, followed by concentration on education of both less able

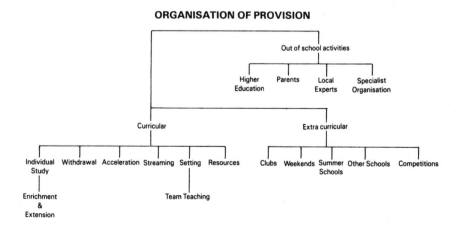

**Figure 4.2**

and the more able as exemplars of similarities and differences in need and strategies in provision.

Once a teacher has been teaching for a while in school, then is the time to build on that essential experience to study in greater depth by in-service courses and higher degrees the needs of our most able children.

*Teaching strategies*

The implementation of appropriate and specific strategies in the regular classroom will form a solid basis for the education of gifted and talented students, and some of these issues have already been discussed.

Grouping is providing various organisational structures of either long or short duration, whereby students of a like ability can work together. One of these categories is full time homogeneous grouping, such as the magnet schools in the US, where students of various ability levels are taken to the particular school that accommodates their needs and career interests. Another category is commonly called cluster grouping and involves placing a group of gifted students in the same regular class for special assignments and field trips. This could mean that the regular common core curriculum may be compacted to allow time for enrichment activities.

In some countries, of course, there are special schools for the gifted as in America and Israel. In the UK we have the famous Choir Schools, the Royal Ballet School and the Yehudi Menuhin School of Music, to name but a few. However, on the whole, we do not believe in this country in segregating children for ideological reasons.

Indeed, for the same reasons, we have tended to teach in mixed ability groups and here, the teacher has to be an excellent manager and disciplinarian in order to make sure that children reach the higher potential of which they are capable. Mixed ability grouping was, in part, a reaction to the rigid banding and streaming that existed in most of our schools.

Streaming is certainly one organisational method of creating a situation which is in danger of hinging around quantity rather than trying to create qualitatively different kind of work. It is, however, based on the theory that peoples who are of a certain ability in one area are, therefore, of a similar ability in most areas. This is most outdated and a disproven theory. Whereas setting, while being an improvement on the above, has many drawbacks, as well as some benefits. Primary school teachers in England seem to provide work of a more advanced nature to the top set in any one class, which should be appropriate to meeting the needs of those intellectual characteristics mentioned earlier. The work carried out in sets or bands is usually too rigid, too structured and lacking in open-ended problem solving elements so needed to allow the potential of highly able children to flourish.

It is suggested that a process-centred approach is an alternative one to adopt with very able children. If we can identify those higher-level intellectual abilities and talents, then it is these that would form the basis of any enrichment or extension work with very able children.

Organisationally, such work could be designed to fit into normal school lessons, with the most able working on this kind of material in the same classroom as the rest of the class, who will proceed with their usual work. Alternatively, the most able could be withdrawn, some from their usual lessons, as in remedial education to attend some process-centred sessions. This imaginative and stimulating approach tries to provide some qualitatively different work for the very able. We must remember, however, that not just the very able are capable of using these higher level intellectual skills, as process-centred work should form part of the curriculum for every child. The other concern is that much of the package material available for such children is still teacher-directed, lacking in the provision of opportunities for open-ended problem solving and investigation and is all too often carried out in much the same way as other school work.

Experience has shown that students of similar ability levels work well together despite age differences and the scheduling of some class time should be allowed for this type of activity. The time may be used for tutorial time work, with the older student instructing or leading the younger intellectual peer. Projects should be co-operative in nature, with students of different grades who have similar interests or strengths, being grouped to pursue a selected topic. Such a grouping would allow for the efficient use of the resources necessary.

## Mentorship

Teachers should be humble enough to realise that it is not always possible to extend the children we have been discussing to their ultimate and that there are numerous people in the community who would be delighted to help in various ways. For example, a student could be matched up with a person who has been made redundant who has a similar enthusiasm and ability for a certain topic or subject. These community resources are available, and where curriculum compacting has been achieved, this mentorship model can provide a very worthwhile learning experience for able children. A typical scenario will be where an adult member of the community and a single student meet regularly over a period of months, with the student possibly visiting the mentor at the job site to learn first-hand and in detail, the activities, responsibilities, problems and lifestyle associated with a particular business, profession or art. Of course, mentorship presumes a commitment on the part of the student and the mentor to plan a detailed sequence of learning activities designed to achieve a specified goal.

## Counselling

Some of the children we have been discussing and their parents as well, would benefit from counselling, which would provide a support system for gifted and talented students and pay attention to the social and emotional well-being, as well as the academic means. Every effort should be made to improve the well-being of students through the provision of help with normal developmental tasks, as well as the special problems associated with being gifted. The obvious problem is that of dealing with expectations, as some of these students find their level of achievement which they should be attaining in conflict with those of their parents and teachers. For example, some female children continue to have difficulty in making decisions about taking courses in non-traditional career areas in mathematics.

The students could be helped with skills involved in studying and management of time. One challenge to any school is to identify the talent pool of staff, because teachers have hidden interests just like our children. Other areas within a school where counselling could take place would be in small tutorial groups, or a few minutes in the lunchtime or after school with a teacher who has a like interest with that of the gifted child. Ideally, each school should have a counsellor, who would be part of the school team, consulting the classroom teachers, encouraging the use of peer group dynamics to re-enforce student co-operation. This goes on in most of our schools in the area of career counselling and these should start early, as indicated ealier in this text. These children need assistance in defining career goals and identifying appropriate ways early in their school careers.

Counselling is an important element in any gifted education programme, but staffing levels in British schools are not usually good enough to cope. It is hoped that one day, we shall have a counsellor appointed to at least every secondary school, as happens in North America.

The tutorial system in British schools is a sporadic one and needs a coherent plan, as many gifted and talented children need support. They may have personal and social concerns, as well as educational and careers decisions to make. Parents and teachers can support one another here to help their children discover interests and abilities and to relate these to lifestyle, educational and career opportunities. There is often a need for family counselling, as some parents are bewildered, disbelieving, fearful, or even resentful of their child's abilities. The NAGC Counselling Service is recommended to both parents and schools.

As we discussed earlier, career development is one of the few areas of provision which is supported by research (Shore, 1991). Career counselling helps children to mark career possibilities early and should favour those open-ended ones that allow for further challenge and growth. This is vital for the broadly gifted child who is good at everything and yet, having gained 10 'A' grades at GCSE has to make a decision about 'A' levels.

Some parents put considerable pressure on their children to follow in the family business, or to go into a career that does not coincide with their child's true desire. Girls in particular may need convincing that career and family are compatible, and children from poor backgrounds and some ethnic groups may need their sights setting higher. Professional models from similar disadvantaged backgrounds can be a vital component of a successful career service.

### Flexible progression

This involves the promotion of a child to a level of study beyond that which is usual for his or her age group. It may take the form of earlier enrolment, early completion of a stage and entry to the next stage in one or more subjects, and even earlier entry to tertiary education.

### Extra-mural activities

In most countries now there are special summer schools and Saturday classes where courses of study are provided in one or more areas for gifted and talented students. The students are able to pursue knowledge and skills with other students of superior ability, and this has been shown to be a stimulating experience for them. With their staff of experts, many colleges and universities would be delighted to help and meet a child or group of children who have a fascination for a particular subject (Endean and George, 1982).

### Using the library more efficiently

It is essential that we ensure that students receive their full entitlement to books and literature. Someone has wisely said that 'a blessed companion is a book'. It is the work of everyone in education, and not just teachers, to shape and be inspired by strong and sound values and give our pupils a chance of acquiring, and hopefully living by, those values. In these days of economic stringency, this, in a very vital sense, would give the country value for money, as an investment in values will provide just the kind of return we need.

Trevor Dickinson HMI, at a recent conference, stressed that it is important to see the National Curriculum as a framework, and to build for children a rich educational experience around it. In particular, he stressed that literature offers joy, creativity, the chance for children to see as others see, to feel as others feel and to move beyond narrow confines of space and time. Literature also demands that readers ask vital questions about life and living and in this sense, literature and poetry are important prompts to thought. They are also powerful aids to growth and language confidence. It is, however, not just the availability of good literature, but the use the children make of good literature, including reference material in the library. There are skills to be taught here so that children can research a project on their own and be aware of literature retrieval methodologies which can be found in any good library.

*Local organisation*

Many local organisations such as the Royal Society for the Protection of Birds and the Local History Society, often have junior membership and this can be a good outlet for students whose enthusiasm and abilities exceed the regularly offered course work.

(1)    Computer technology has great potential for individualised learning and this could provide a valuable additional tool to be used in enrichment programmes for these children. The skill of languages, such as Basic, Lozo and Pascal, should be taught at an early age and can be used to generate ideas. Some children are capable of developing their own software and design their own technologies.

(2)    Children can learn a great deal about the lifestyle of mentors and problems of industry, commerce and the professions, as well as acting as a role model. It is important to carefully match the mentor to the child; have a clear plan of objectives and evaluate progress carefully. Ideally, double mentoring is recommended, whereby a mentor from the community is shadowed by a professional teacher to ensure development is progressive. This may involve regular in-school and after-school meetings.

(3)    Secondary schools and summer camps are increasingly popular and have the advantage of permitting gifted children to meet like-minded children away from the restrictions of a busy school life. Most Saturday schools are run by NAGC in Britain, or by a higher education institution, and are taught by volunteer specialist teachers, lecturers or community experts, assisted by parents of the gifted child. Normally the children attending are selected by teachers whose children would benefit from being extended and the programmes designed to be inclusive and not exclusive (Endean and George, 1982; Davis and Rimm, 1989).

As we stated earlier, when discussing mentoring and the importance of good parenting, the most time-consuming and sensitive task is that of matching students to mentors. The school cannot expect to do everything themselves, teaching is too demanding, and therefore, the talent pool of the community is a vital resource. The School Co-ordinator for gifted and talented children should seek out members of the community from all walks of life, not only willing to share their expertise with children, but also time, patience and understanding. The success of the programme for each child hinges on an effective match.

A suggested approach to the community for support in this area is shown below.

**Community Resource Survey**
**To Parents and Friends of the School**

We now have a policy in the school for supporting our most able children and are looking for volunteers to share their knowledge and experience with our children. We are aware that our community is represented by many professions, trades, vocations, as well as hobbies and interests. If you are willing to support us in this way, then we would appreciate it if you would complete this form and return it to the school as soon as possible.

Name.................................... Address ..................................

Occupation............................. ..................................

Business Tel. No..................... Home Tel. No.........................

Below are areas which could supplement the curriculum for your children and help to extend them in order to help them reach their full potential. Please complete the form by indicating what you could offer, e.g. talk, practical demonstration, written materials, visual aids or displays:

*Sciences:*
Biology
Conservation
Geology
Chemistry
Astronomy
etc.

*Social Sciences:*
Travel
Geography
History
Economics
Sociology
etc.

*Professions/Trades:*
Doctor
Para-medics
Nursing
Law
Vet
Plumber
Policeman
Engineer
etc.

*General:*
Arts, Crafts
Music
Literature
Business
Languages
Social Work
Journalism
Insurance
etc.

*Hobbies:*
Photography
Stamps
Music
Painting
Fishing
Gardening
Model Making
Horses
etc.

90

A further aid to motivate these children is to provide them with a contract worksheet each week and the following is a typical example which is recommended.

# Contract Worksheet

The following is an example of a basic contract form on which pupils clarify tasks to be completed within a self-organised time frame. A series of questions guide them in the assessment of their work behaviours.

PUPIL TASK SHEET

| Date/time | *Task to be worked on*<br>(state clearly *what* you intend<br>to do and *when*) | Checklist/work due<br>(list ongoing tasks and<br>when they are due) |

——SUITABLE SPACE LEFT
HERE——

**EVALUATION – How well did you work?**          M   T   W   T   F

 1. I moved quietly and settled to my tasks quickly
 2. I listened carefully and followed the instructions
 3. I worked quietly not disturbing others
 4. I planned and organised my time well
 5. I used my spare time wisely
 6. I completed my tasks giving thought and effort
 7. I participated in discussion groups
 8. I proof-read and checked my work before handing in
 9. I corrected any errors and added words to my learning list
10. I thought about neat handwriting/presentation
11. I worked well unsupervised
12. I handed in and collected my work daily

*Acceleration*

Any teaching strategy that results in advanced placement beyond a child's chronological age is titled acceleration and this is the most popular way to cope with more able childlren in Britain (NAGC, 1990a). The Act assumes that most children will reach attainment targets six or seven, but also that some will reach nine or ten. Thus the Act recognises able children who may reach this level. However, there is little cognisance of the wide abilities found in any one class of children, nor of their different needs and the curriculum context is the same for all.

The subject has been studied extensively and research has supported its use with these children (Gold, 1979). Brody and Benbow (1987) noted that acceleration offers students the opportunity to select a programme of work that is both challenging and interesting. It is also helpful to the school because /a special programme does not have to be developed and implemented for such children.\ Able children should certainly have the opportunity to work at their own rapid pace, to progress through and out of primary school on into the secondary phase and beyond. Acceleration which speeds up learning time to match students potential and capabilities is to be welcomed.

With early admission to the infant school, careful screening should be encouraged. They should be intellectually precocious, reasonable at motor co-ordination, have good health, social maturity and possess adequate reading skills. Early admission to the junior and secondary phases of education will benefit children who are ready for a more specialised course, but it will probably mean abandoning friends.

There are, however, critics of this approach and they warn of its potential problems. Coleman (1985) suggests that acceleration resulted in teaching the same material, only teaching it faster. He also suggests that it can lead to emotional and social maladjustment.

The majority of the literature does not support this latter point (Whitmore, 1981; Birch et al., 1965), but nevertheless, it is a crucial decision to make. Teachers and parents are referred to the following check list which should be carefully considered before accelerating a child, a step which may be irreversible. For example, not all children progress steadily through their school career and if a child's development slows, it could cause feelings of failure and frustration. Perhaps most important of all are the differing rates of a child's emotional and social development *vis-à-vis* academic growth. A child could find herself in an atmosphere, having left friends behind, which is not inducive to personal growth and development. This is potentially a situation which can lead to difficulties in the development of her ability to make good social relationships and to consequent long-term unhappiness. The risk can be considerably tempered when acceleration is modified to part time attendance in a higher class for a child's specific talent area. Examples of this practice are John Hopkins University in the US and the Royal Institution Maths and Science master classes in London and elsewhere. Vernon *et al* (1977) give evidence that adverse effects can be minimalised when the following criteria are carefully judged for each child.

The child is adequately prepared psychologically
The teachers of the new classes are sensitive and aware

The child is both emotionally and physically mature
The child is not accelerated more than one year
The child really is capable of advanced work

By allowing a very able child to jump some of the normal school curriculum by moving into an older class, it is hoped that a child will be more stimulated, less bored and enjoy school better. It is also the easiest administrative way out of the problem.

Above all, we need to emphasise that all programmes must be designed to produce sensible, defensible and valuable educational goals.

## Acceleration or promotion

*Check list of criteria to be met for consideration of early promotion:*

(To be used more as safeguard than rigidly)

(1)  Attainments well above average for age.
(2)  Evidence of exceptional ability from tests and performance.
(3)  Emotional and social maturity for age.
(4)  Can cope with physical activities with reasonable motor co-ordination.
(5)  Anxiety and perseverance at reasonable level without evidence of stress or obsessional behaviour.
(6)  Parental agreement and support.
(7)  School agreement and support.
(8)  Readiness of child to separate from friendship group. Are older friends already established?

*Factors to be borne in mind:*

(1)  A decision made at eight years old can rarely be changed later – repeating a year later on is bad for morale.
(2)  Child may be functioning five years in advance, not just one – marginal benefit?
(3)  Impact on other children in family.
(4)  Classroom organisation and policy in the school, e.g. all age groups, large ranges of ability.

*The benefits of a 'second opinion' e.g. school education psychologist*

(1)  To confirm that the child has exceptional abilities unlike others in the peer group and that this has been consistent.
(2)  To confirm that the child has the necessary emotional maturity.
(3)  To confirm that the social integration is likely to be successful.

(4)   To consider the long-term consequences.

(5)   To protect the child from over-ambitious parent or teacher.

(6)   To check that the child is not being used to fulfil the needs of an adult.

(7)   To protect the teachers from parental pressure and ill-will.

(8)   To give parents access to professional advice that can continue when the child has left the present school.

*Points for discussion*

(1)   What important differences are there between the highly gifted child and a 'great' man or woman?

(2)   In what sense can we say that the difference between a highly gifted child and a bright, able child is as great or greater than the difference between that bright able child and a child of average abilities?

(3)   Why does the meeting of needs of a gifted or talented child in terms of equality of opportunity mean unequal treatment?

(4)   Is this additional and/or different treatment ethically sound when all that can be done is not being done for children with 'negative' rather than 'positive' handicaps?

(5)   How can the general class teachers who are often outstripped in intellect and skills by gifted and talented youngsters best cope with them and with their own inadequacies?

(6)   Elitist intellectual groups seem ruled out by our social philosophy; is there a place in this country for specialist schools each to encourage a particular talent, for example art, ballet, music, along with a general education? (As for example in Russia, Israel and to a lesser extent in this country.) We do, after all, have a few specialist schools and indeed, we have been extracting children for special activities for some time, for example music, where we have peripatetic specialist incidentally, and certainly games.

(7)   If the answer to 6 is YES, then what about science and maths? And then, where do you draw the line?

# CHAPTER 5

# Enriching the Curriculum

> Do not believe in a fate that falls on men however they act; but I do believe in a fate that falls on men unless they act. (G. K. Chesterton)

> They are able because they think they are able. (Virgil)

> It's not my gratitude but my attitude that will determine my attitude. (Jesse Jackson).

There are many variations in the interpretation of the term 'enrichment', although most people find common ground in the inclusion of a number of ideas. This was recognised by Ogilvie (1973) when he stated that ' "enrichment" will mean different things to different people, and represents something of an amalgam in the minds of us all'. It is defined in the DES glossary as: 'General term for a change in quality of work to a level much higher than that normally expected of a particular age group. Enrichment materials purport to promote or support a higher level of thinking.'

> Those who teach mathematics must take into account the great variation which exists between pupils both in their rate of learning and also in their level of attainment at any age. It follows that mathematics courses must be matched both in level and pace to the needs of pupils; and therefore, a 'differentiated curriculum' must be provided so that pupils will be enabled to develop to the full their mathematical skill and understanding, a positive attitude towards mathematics, and confidence in making use of it.
>
> (Kingman Report)

Reports from many sources have commented upon the disturbing evidence relating to able children and the work which they are asked to do. The following extracts illustrate the point:

> In almost all the cases where work was not reasonably matched to children's capabilities, it was insufficiently demanding. It was very rare for children in any age or ability group to be required to undertake work which was too difficult for them.
>
> (DES, 1978)

> In a large minority of cases, teachers' expectations of what pupils could achieve are clouded by inadequate knowledge and understanding of each pupil's aptitudes and difficulties; teaching is frequently directed at the middle level of ability so that the most able pupils are understretched and the least able cannot cope. (DES, 1985b)

This particular comment concerned secondary schools.

> There is, however, a good deal of evidence from the survey to suggest that more able pupils need more opportunities and stimulus to pursue their own initiatives'. (DES, 1979, Ch 6)

## *Enrichment – definition accepted by the Oxford Research Project (1985)*

(1) Is a broadening and deepening of the learning experience.
(2) Provides experiences and activities beyond the regular curriculum.
(3) Develops the intellectual gifts and talents of the most able.
(4) Stresses qualitative development of thinking skills rather than quantitive accumulation of facts.
(5) Emphasises the process of learning rather than content.
(6) Can be horizontal, exploring bodies of knowledge that are not frequently touched upon in the school common core curriculum.
(7) Can be vertical developing the skill of quantitive thinking which implies a facility with subject matter and ability to understand basic principles and to make generalisations.
(8) Generally these children should do less and learn more. For example, it is generally preferable for a pupil to find three possible solutions to a problem than to solve three problems of a similar nature.

(George, 1985)

## Curriculum for the gifted and talented

All our enrichment activities should be planned and designed with the following objectives in mind (Davis and Rimm, 1989):

Maximum achievement in basic skills
Content beyond the National Curriculum
Exposure to a variety of fields of study
Student selected content
High content complexity
Creative thinking and problem solving
Development of thinking skills
Attentive development
Motivation

It seems logical to consider enrichment and differentiated work together, as the concept of enrichment leads directly to differentiated work. Most teachers provide a measure of enrichment work by writing suitable work-sheets, modifying text and encouraging children to read widely. As seen above, however, the process of enrichment is more than a simple provision of more demanding materials. Enrichment is an activity which is a function of the teacher's flexibility, sensitivity and individual needs, a sense of timing and a mastery of subject area.

Planned interaction with other able pupils should be a part of any individual's enrichment programme, and teachers should consciously direct the study programme of each individual pupil so that he or she must know when to enter into a dialogue with the pupil and when to inject new material of suitable variety.

As we have seen above, enrichment and extension of all pupils is important. There is often a mismatch between the work that is given to able pupils and what they are capable of doing. An observant teacher will note that some children cope easily with the work set and will need to make greater demands so that interest and enthusiasm are not lost. Butler-Por (1987) in her excellent book on underachievers quotes the following poem which is a sad indictment on some teachers:

'To Learn the Bible'

Today I am so happy
Today I am going to learn
How the world was created.
How the world was chaos,
And by God's hand changed.
I shall start to study diligently,
I shall be an industrious pupil.
Now I am so happy –
I shall learn how things began

Three weeks later, Inbal wrote in her diary:

To learn the Bible is awful,
All the time to listen
All the time to write and hear
A story I think did not happen.
O how terrible to learn everything by heart.
To read it to the teacher, nicely.
I wish the Bible will not be taught –
For each story to be repeated twice!

Here we have a naturally curious child who had a need to discover and understand. This is a strong intrinsic, motivational force in any child's learning. Inbal had encouraging, urging and fulfilling experiences at home, and hoped this would continue at school, but the teacher succeeded in killing her initial curiosity in an area of learning that held so much promise for this child of seven. Hopefully, some future teacher will re-kindle her interest and enthusiasm. The Collins dictionary (1986) defines enrichment as 'increase the wealth of, to endow with fine or desirable qualities, to enrich one's experience, improve in quality, to enhance, to make more productive'. Enrichment, then, can be any type of activity which is outside the core of learning which most pupils undertake that is over and above the core National Curriculum subjects. Eyre and Marjoram (1990) state that

> enrichment is a process by which school work becomes alive and exciting, and by which learning is an organic, growing, never-ending, but ever-fascinating journey. It is not about perfunctory completion of routine tasks, but about enlarging horizons, tackling problems whose solutions give rise to further problems, seeking peaks, experimenting with new materials, processes and ideas. It is also about enhancing the quality of life in the classroom and heightening sensitivity.

In this philosophical and idealistic statement, it is challenging for any teacher to consider how they match up in what they provide for their children.

Here are some of the questions we should all ask ourselves:

(1)    To what extent is the work we give our children individualised and designed for the more able of a group?

(2)    Do our worksheets allow for variations in the quality of thinking, or do gifted children merely finish more quickly than the rest of the class?

(3)    What techniques do we use to set differentiated work? Do we set differentiated tasks? Do the tasks really present new challenges, or just 'more of the same'?

(4)    To what extent do we use whole class methods and how do they challenge the gifted child?

(5)    Are potential developments of a topic adequately resourced? Now all of us complain about the lack of resources, but we are the most important, expensive resource of any school and perhaps we should also consider what is already available in our school by looking at our stockbooks and seeing what equipment has been accumulated over the years.

(6)    How often do we offer suggestions for further reading which utilises our vocabulary or concepts well above the levels used in whole class teaching?

(7)    Do we promote a policy of differentiated homework? Is this desirable? Possibly homework is the best example of individualisation of the curriculum we have available to us. It should be a standard practice insofar as sets are given differentiated howework, but is there need for more careful differentiation?

These are challenging times, and these are challenging questions. With teacher appraisal on the horizon, we should at least ask ourselves these questions and others, if we are to be given the status of being truly professional. Basic questions should be asked at the end of every day by every teacher. What have I done today? What have the children done today? What have the children learnt today? What have I learnt today? How have the children and I spent our time? How many questions did we allow the children to ask today? The same dictionary gives a definition of extension as 'to draw out, or to be drawn out, to broaden the scope or meaning, to widen, to stretch or expand'. This implies that children move through the curriculum at a different pace and is a process of moving to a higher level of skill or more difficult concept. The two terms, extension and enrichment, seem to overlap and they are often used interchangeably and synonomously, but should not be seen as the same thing. They have different aims and functions in the classroom, with enrichment meaning to broaden horizons and experience of our children and extension, to move our children to higher order skills, concepts and attitudes.

The National Curriculum emphasises that the curriculum for all children should have breadth and depth, as well as balance and relevance, and all this cannot be provided by the National Curriculum alone. We need to constantly remind ourselves that the National Curriculum is a foundation to be augmented by additional subjects, cross-curricula themes, dimensions and skills and extra-curricula activities. The vision for the more able child must be made within this framework (Curriculum Guidance 3). Descriptions of school subjects embodied in legislation are not intended to be exhaustive, and enrichment programmes must draw on a broader conceptualisation of the subjects. For example, able pupils have many opportunities within the recently-published technology order, which contains little content as such, but gives children and teachers the opportunity to develop their own ideas. Primary pupils will have the opportunity to work uninterrupted for a day or two on activities which have a design in technology focus, whereas in secondary schools, design and technology activities will typically extend over half a term. It is essential that careful consideration be given to both the whole curriculum and the individual subject curriculum for the above child. For pupils with an uneven profile across attainment levels, can breadth be sacrificed for part of a key stage to allow for specialisation in certain attainment targets, provided a scheme of work across the key stage as a whole is balanced? See Appendix for description of the National Curriculum. Although it is permissable to move pupils up or down a key stage, groups or schools may be exempted from part or all of National Curriculum requirements. It is not needed, since the key stage is defined by the average of the group; the value of doing this needs careful consideration. Such pupils might gain more by remaining with their peers and being given the benefit of a broader range of learning context, innovative teaching methods and greater flexibility in learning approaches. This should include the use of self-supported study in the same subject, but where the material is broader than that suggested in the attainment targets specified by law. Extended work experience may be of enormous benefit to older pupils, as would the provision of tasks which address real problems and issues.

The National Association for Curriculum Enrichment has written a number of individual learning kits which will enable a gifted child on occasions, to work on their own, at their own pace, and to be semi-independent of a busy teacher. These materials have been written to provide genuine enrichment over and above the National Curriculum materials and to enable children to go as far and as fast as they can without any brakes being put on them.

Where pupils do work outside their key stage, careful consideration has to be given to the age appropriateness of schemes of work where levels of maturity of the pupil on the one hand and the curriculum content on the other, may be mis-matched. If a decision is taken for a pupil to work in the next key stage, it may be difficult to find programmes of study at the right level in all subjects. Whereas, in mathematics, for example, programmes of study are level related, in science, they are key stage related. Readers will recall that these are essential subjects for gifted and talented children.

If a pupil is to work for most of the time on programmes of study from the next key stage and remain in his or her peer group, disapplication will be required. However, when would the decision be made to disapply? Take key stages 3 and 4 for example; if the level of achievement for a subject is not to be assigned to a pupil until the end of the key stage, the teacher could make provision for the next key stage without disapplication from the range of levels, whilst keeping the pupil in his or her peer group. However, there will be some pupils who might – in mathematics for example – achieve levels 7 or 8 by the end of key stage 2; they would start key stage 3 only just within the range of levels 3–8, and would, therefore, have every expectation of starting key stage 4 work before the end of key stage 3. Disapplication from the key stage 3 range of levels in this case would seem likely if the pupil was to continue working with key stage 3 peers.

National Curriculum Council has already expressed the view that the option of Special Educational Needs pupils working with younger pupils in an earlier key stage will not often be practicable or desirable. Does the same argument hold for pupils working with older pupils from the next key stage? An alternative may be withdrawal of exceptionally able pupils for individual provision for part of the week.

The legislation takes into account the special circumstances of vertically grouped primary classes where the head teacher can assign pupils to a key stage according to an individual's age, rather than according to the age of the majority in the class. This facility in primary schools does not, however, facilitate accelerated progression, where this is deemed appropriate, without, apparently, the need for disapplication because of its adherence to designation of key stage by age rather than by levels of achievement. This aspect of the legislation may impede consideration of pupil-groupings that are other than age-related.

It is likely that enrichment programmes associated with each attainment level will be developed from amplification, elaboration and extension of the programmes of study at the same level of attainment rather than the next level of attainment. Enrichment programmes of various kinds should benefit all pupils from the most to the least able.

Paragraph 8.40 of the recently published History Working Group report makes special reference to gifted pupils: 'We recommend that gifted pupils should be given access to, and encouragement to acquire, supplementary historical information and understanding relating to the History Study Unit in hand and be given tasks which will fully stretch their ability.' There are over 40 detailed History Study Units of various kinds described in the History Working Group final report; all are key stage rather than level-related.

NCC has been asked to consider extension courses and curriculum options for pupils who reach level 10 or achieve goods GCSEs in English, mathematics, science or technology before the end of key stage 4. An NCC Task Group is considering extension studies in mathematics and science; some possibilities being considered are: additional Attainment Targets and Programmes of Study beyond level 10; progression to A and AS level at end of Year 10; new, post-GCSE qualifications (possibly undertaken by independent study) and certificated at GCSE (subjects such as astronomy, horticulture).

ATs 2 and 3 in science and the four design and technology ATs might be combined into a biotechnology course. For the very able minority of pupils who wish to spend extra time on other subjects, Model B, covering 10 rather than 17 ATs, is a reduced, though nevertheless conceptually challenging course.

NCC has already recommended that, if high achievers at 14 in science wish to study more science, they could start a Triple Award enhanced Model A balanced course in Year 10, or undertake a Double Award course in Year 10 followed by an enhanced balanced science course for a third GCSE at the end of Year 11. The Council has strongly recommended that all pupils study Double Award Science and that any extension studies should be for balanced, not single-subject science.

The core subjects, technology and modern foreign language, must be studied to 16. Still to be determined are the levels at which pupils move to extension work in these subjects. Given the demanding nature of design and technology, few pupils are likely to take an early GCSE in this subject.

NCC is also considering the relationship between levels attained at the end of key stage 3 and levels attained by those permitted to move to extension studies at the end of Year 10.

NCC is additionally giving thought to the circumstances in which pupils might drop the other foundation subjects before the end of key stage 4. The Secretary of State has suggested level 8, which would prevent widespread 'dropping' and thereby enhance the status of such subjects within the National Curriculum as a whole. They remain strongly 'an entitlement'. The argument against level 8 is that the small numbers entitled to drop a subject would make special curricular provision impractical.

Level 7 would open this up to a large number of pupils but this level might be thought too low a level of attainment for a foundation subject to be dropped.

Some of the options available for pupils who drop subjects will be: to begin work of an A/AS type; to study another subject in the same curricular area, for example statistics; to study a course in the same subject taken to a greater depth or breadth. However, pupils who have been very successful in a subject may not wish to drop it at the end of Year 10 in order to start another subject. A pilot monitoring study is currently under way and a main evaluation programme has begun.

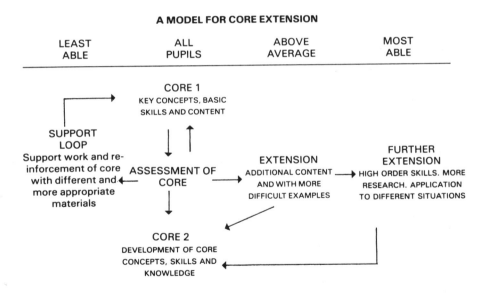

**A MODEL FOR CORE EXTENSION**

Figure 5.1

## Differentiation

Differentiation has become a buzz word, a convenient portfolio term for an issue which has always been with us. HMI reports have frequently drawn attention to the scandal of undifferentiated lessons. The concept is relatively simple, but is not like learning a new trick in order to get it right. It is a word like creativity and enrichment that trips off the tongue of many of us daily and means different things to different people. Creating the conditions to achieve it is a difficult task and differentiation for all, its common currency, is an illusive goal. The word keeps surfacing because the detailed practice to produce it is so hard to sustain and the solutions to the problem are very challenging. Even when the goal seems within our reach, something may happen which turns the apparent success into an illusion.

Schools and colleges should offer children a basic entitlement to a broad range of curriculum experiences. However, the differences in pupils' natural abilities and interests mean their individual needs will differ as they progress through this curriculum. To provide for their basic entitlement, pupils in the same group must have learning opportunities matched to their particular needs and abilities. The process of assessing individual needs and responding with appropriate learning experiences is called differentiation.

A curriculum which is differentiated for every pupil will: build on past achievements; present challenges to allow for more achievements; provide opportunity for success; and remove barriers to participation. This means teachers devising tasks appropriate to the range of abilities, aptitudes and interests of their children, regularly reviewing pupils' progress through observation, discussion and testing, which leads to variation in the tasks pupils have to undertake, and then teachers offering support for individual work, both in person and through the ready availability of appropriate resources. This word differentiation has become a live issue because schools experience difficulty in coping effectively with the wide range of pupils that come through their doors. The spread of comprehensive schools and the increasing access to mainstream schools of pupils who have quite acute learning or behavioural difficulties, has highlighted an issue that has always been there. The mixed ability groups, taken for granted and on the whole, well executed in primary schools, are seen by some as a threat to standards in the secondary school. There has been a long running debate about standards, which shows no sign of diminishing. For some, the solution lies in the return to grammar schools, which for those who thrived in them were often a great success, but there was also a great deal of underachievement in the old tripartite system, just as there undoubtedly is in many a comprehensive school today. To link differentiation to pupils at the extremes of the normal distribution curve of ability is to miss the point. No mass of 60 per cent of our pupils in the middle range are doing well in our schools. Some are, but many are not. Differentiation is not primarily about helping slow learners or disaffected pupils. Differentiation is not just about stretching the clever child. Differentiation is about all children, because all children are different, and one of the fascinating aspects of being a teacher is this very fact of human variation and all its attributes. Differentiation then is the process by which curriculum objectives, teaching methods, assessment methods, resources and learning activities are planned to cater for the needs of individual pupils. Differentiation is accessing the whole curriculum to the

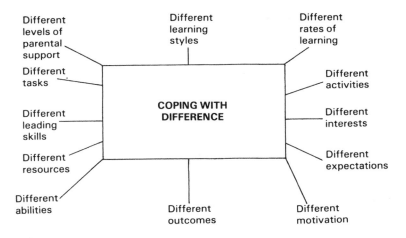

**Figure 5.2**

learning needs of the individual. This is as good a definition as any. With this definition in mind, it then becomes the linchpin of the entitlement curriculum. It is meaningless if access is not available. The other important point about this definition is the emphasis on the individual, and this could prove to be a much more helpful emphasis in categories like slow learner, average, bright or gifted, although it would be foolish to suggest that these categories are meaningless. They are all marked by individuality, and our children think differently, they behave differently, they learn differently, they come from different backgrounds and they bring different skills, attitudes and abilities with them. This is both the joy, but also the great challenge for the busy teacher. For this reason, I regard differentiation as an issue affecting all pupils of every age in every kind of school in every kind of grouping, for this is what makes the teaching profession such a skilled pursuit. Figure 5.2 summarises some of these differences.

Teachers use two major ways of differentiating learning activities. The first is commonly called differentiation by task. After establishing curriculum objectives for a class activity, the next step is to develop tasks which help individual pupils achieve these objectives. There are many factors which affect the difficulty of the task, and these include:

- The required accuracy for measurements.
- How familiar the pupils are with the materials and apparatus to be used.
- How familiar the pupils are with the concepts and vocabulary involved in the investigation.
- The extent to which a teacher leads or prompts pupils.
- The number and types of variables involved in any investigation.

Secondly, there is differentiation by outcomes. This involves setting a common task for the class. The task is designed so that every pupil understands what is required of them. They use their knowledge and understanding to achieve success at different levels. The more able should be expected to:

- Plan and carry out more complex work.
- Use more difficult concepts in planning their work.
- Make more accurate measurements.
- Complete more stages in an investigation.
- Record results more precisely.
- Express findings in more sophisticated vocabulary.

**Table 5.1:** Effective teaching styles which assist differentiation

Humour
Praise
Positive attitude and high expectations
Responsive to pupil ideas
Clear organisation
Clear instructions and objectives set
Resources available
Teacher allows time for pupils to reflect
Teacher intervenes to check progress
Teacher intervenes to diagnose difficulties
Teacher intervenes to move work forward
Teacher resists over-demanding pupil
Teacher finds opportunities to create a 'community of learning' in the classroom – some whole class work and group work and other teaching strategies.
Teacher varies length of tasks to provide:
  (a)  some long, open-ended opportunities enabling all the work at their own pace.
  (b)  complete opportunities so that reflection/completion/feedback are all within a short period.
Teacher involves pupils by explaining objectives, work plan, expected outcomes, success and assessment criteria – giving pupils opportunity to plan the pathway, through their own work and anticipate the difficulties of different pupils.
Result from detailed planning (preferably in collaboration with others).
Teacher gives short crisp demonstrations/punchy introductions.
Teacher sets varied and realistic timescales for the work.
Teacher should have planned support, consolidation and extension activities.
Teacher keeps up-to-date records, to identify what children have achieved and where to move next.

The emphasis should be on effective teaching styles which assist a creative learning environment, in which differentiation is most likely to happen (see Tables 5.1 and 5.2).

**Table 5.2:** The learning environment in which differentiation is most likely to happen

Arises from a fully planned workscheme to which a team of people have contributed.
Differentiation as an issue as highlighted by format of workscheme eg. column on a grid, the special needs of slow learners and able pupils are planned for in advance.
Teaching/learning approaches are an integral part of the planned scheme.
A wide variety of teaching/learning styles is deployed (see Table 5.1).
Students are involved in the planning of their work.
Active steps are taken to organise the room and to manage the situation to minimise low level demands on teacher by pupils. Give pupils ready access to their current work, both storage and wall displays.
Teacher actively seeks opportunities to know pupils and their work.
Assessment is linked to the aims/objectives of workscheme. Students are aware of success criteria. Teacher's recording methods reflect wide range of assessment opportunities.
Control is fully established so that the efforts of all are directed to the planned task.
Comfortable atmosphere – humour, praise, positive enthusiastic attitude on part of teacher – defined by one colleague as 'cheerfulness'.
Independent learning is encouraged.
Mixture of open-ended and limited time tasks, latter requiring a specific outcome.
Wide range of stimulating, easily and independently accessible resources: print, pictures, videos, artifacts which lead to creative, reflective, speculative response appropriate to the range of ability encompassed within the class.

On this point of vocabulary, there follows a typical short scheme of work based on tree studies which are commonly used for children's investigations in the environment, whether it is in a city park, or rural village school. However, many children are capable of much more advanced language which should be encouraged in every subject, and in this case, in science. The question, therefore, is which of the words from the two tables would one use?

In order to implement enrichment, extension and a differentiated curriculum in the classroom, we must remember that all students learn in many different ways. The wide range of needs of children found in an ordinary classroom is more likely to be met if a wide range of teaching styles is adopted. Not all styles suit all subjects, but many teachers have a narrow repertoire. Teachers are as prone as anyone in any other profession to getting into a rut. Even the best ideas can be overdone and having advocated the individualisation of learning, we must remember that that can be overdone, and it may be that an inspired explanation heard by all and shared by the whole class would be of most benefit.

In an interesting article entitled 'What is Teaching' Paul Hirst (1971) drew an important distinction between the concept of teaching as an enterprise, which included organisational ploys and all the incidentals and necessary preliminaries which a teacher may find himself involved in during the course of a day's work, including sharpening pencils and opening windows, and the concept of teaching as a specific activity which is directly connected to the enhancement of learning. Almost any activity could take on a teaching function. For example, if a teacher was trying to demonstrate certain basic

## TREE STUDIES - SPECIFIC OBJECTIVES

(A) COMPARE DIFFERENCES IN STEM AND BARK STRUCTURE.

(B) DISCOVER HOW TREES ARE RELATED TO OTHER ORGANISMS E.g. BIRDS AND INSECTS.

(C) IDENTIFY AND MAKE A COLLECTION OF THE LEAVES OF TREES.

(D) DEVISE A METHOD OF MEASURING THE HEIGHTS OF TREES

(E) COMPARE SHAPES AND SIZES OF TREES.

(F) RELATE TREES TO USES OF THEIR WOOD.

(G) MAKE A HISTOGRAM OF THE TYPES OF TREES FOUND.

(H) USE A SIMPLE KEY TO IDENTIFY TREE LEAVES, BUDS AND WINTER SILHOUETTES.

(J) COMPARE PLANTS GROWING UNDER TREES WITH THOSE GROWING IN OPEN AREAS.

skills such as how to sharpen pencils, then the performance could be seen as part of a specific teaching activity, but such demonstrations would be marked off from preliminaries of related activities by such remarks as, 'this is the way to do it', or 'if you hold the pencil this way, you can find it easier'. The fresh criteria for genuine teaching is that a teacher must be acting with a clear intention of bringing about learning.

There are, however, two other conditions which must hold if an activity is to be classed as teaching. First the pupils must be learning. The teacher may be undertaking an activity with the intention that the pupils should learn, but if in fact they are not learning, either because they are switched off, or because they have already mastered the skill or item of knowledge already, no teaching is strictly involved. Research shows that this is often the case with gifted and talented children. Secondly, the teacher cannot really be teaching unless what he or she is doing will aid the learning process. To assist a busy teacher in providing the right effective teaching style to aid differentiation, it is most useful to give gifted and talented children the

# USEFUL WORDS FOR EXPRESSING OBJECTIVES

| SIMPLE | MORE COMPLEX |
|---|---|
| IDENTIFY | COMPARE |
| MAKE | DISCRIMINATE |
| DESCRIBE | GENERALISE |
| FIND | DEVISE A METHOD |
| COLLECT | JUSTIFY |
| MEASURE | DISCOVER |
| EXAMINE | FORMULATE HYPOTHESES |
| PREPARE | PROPOSE REASONS FOR |
| CLASSIFY | DEDUCE |
| DRAW | RELATE |
| CONSTRUCT | PROVE |
| ESTIMATE | INFER |
| PLOT A GRAPH | PREDICT |

following learning style inventory, which will then enable you to match how these children learn to what you are able to provide.

*Learning style inventory*

This survey is designed to explore the way you prefer to learn. Look at the four statements in each row and decide how they refer to you. Give four marks for the statement nearest to you, three to the second, two for the third and one for the statement least appropriate to you. There are no right or wrong answers.

| | a | b | c | d |
|---|---|---|---|---|
| 1. | I like to get involved | I like to take my time before acting | I am particular about what I like | I like things to be useful |
| 2. | I like to try things out | I like to analyse things and break them into parts | I am open to new experiences | I like to look at all sides of issues |

3. I like to watch | I like to follow my feelings | I like to be doing things | I like to think about things

4. I accept people and situations the way they are | I like to be aware of what is around me | I like to evaluate | I like to take risks

5. I have gut feelings and hunches | I have a lot of questions | I am logical | I am hard working and get things done

6. I like concrete things, things I can see, feel or touch or smell | I like to be active | I like to observe | I like ideas and theories

7. I prefer learning in here and now | I like to consider and reflect about them | I tend to think about the future | I like to see the results of my work

8. I have to try things out for myself | I rely on my own ideas | I rely on my own observations | I rely on my feelings

9. I am quiet and reserved | I am energetic and enthusiastic | I tend to reason things out | I am responsible about things

Educational reform, which is prevalent throughout the world, is not about allowing able learners to stagnate in an age-grade lock step classroom. If schools were willing to adopt flexible models of grouping that allowed for students' needs to dictate practice, rather than for administrative convenience or fashions of the times, the needs of all children might be better met. If schools were willing to alter instruction based on need as readily as they are willing to move children around administratively, the needs of all children would be better met. Improving the quality of education for all requires that we be sensitive to the needs of all, and plan educational experiences accordingly. Quality of opportunity and quality of treatment in education, however, are not the same, nor should they be. In any profession, the needs of the client dictate the nature of the prescription. While high-quality service should be available to all, the nature and organisation of these services should vary, based on diagnosed need. Education can ill afford to level its services less the bitter pill of mediocrity be absorbed in the bloodstream of all our students.

Educating our most able children in appropriate ways is a challenge that our society must take seriously. We can ill-afford to foster underachievement, disaffection and alienation amongst these children. Even now, national and international comparisons on achievement, drop-out rates, and delinquency data suggest a disproportionately high percentage of our most capable children are not maximising their considerable potential.

# CHAPTER 6

# The Parent/Child/Teacher Model

After you understand about the sun and the stars and the rotation of the earth, you may still miss the radiance of the sunset.        (A. N. Whitehead)

When Michelangelo was going to Rome to see the Pope prior to his being employed to build the Great Dome of St Peters and paint the Sistine Chapel, he took a reference with him which said: 'The bearer of these presents is Michelangelo the sculptor, his nature is such that he requires to be drawn out by kindness and encouragement but if love be shown him and he be treated really well, he will accomplish things that will make the whole world wonder'.

This chapter is primarily for parents who are seen as partners in the educational process with the professionals to make children whole. However, the chapter will be helpful to all concerned in the education of children and, of course, many teachers are parents themselves. It is based on the assumption that children are the most precious natural resource in the world and that parents are the most important teacher a child ever has, particularly in the early crucial years. Parents need to be familiar with the language of education and to know what is going on in schools. If very young children could articulate their feelings, they might well say 'learning about myself and the world around me is my work. Your part is loving and supporting me'. Good parenting then, is an essential part of educating children, but there are some obstacles, risks, challenges, errors and joys that accompany the parent of a child with gifts and talents. This is where it is essential for teachers and parents to be sensitive to each other's problems and help one another.

This chapter will emphasise some practical approaches to the education of gifted and talented children and aims to be different from what has already been written. Please see Painter (1980), Freeman (1985, 1990), White (in Freeman, 1985) and Clarke (1988).

We will begin this discussion by looking at what every child needs. The healthy status of an individual is considered to be governed by the biological integrity and the dynamics of the social cultural factors within the individual's environment. A child's health, due to their dependence, is greatly influenced by the health of the family unit and the qualitative nature of the relationship between members of the family and the wider world. The fact that education has recognised the influence of such factors upon a child's learning is reflected in official educational documents which consistently emphasise the relationships between the child's home, community and school. Space does not allow further discussion on the health of a child, but to remind readers, the World Health Organisation defines health as 'the state of complete physical, mental and social well-being and not merely the absence of disease and infirmity'. With this definition in mind, health is a vital aspect in the total development of all our children, and parents have an important role to play in ensuring that children have adequate sleep, nutrition, exercise and peace of mind.

The interaction of negative emotion and needs of an individual is outlined admirably in Maslow's Hierarchy of Human Needs (1954).

**Figure 6.1**: Maslow's basic human needs

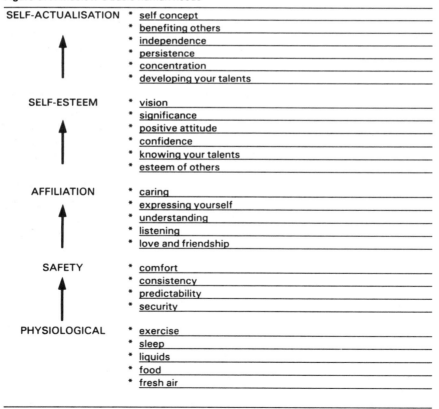

Maslow's model asserts that it is necessary that an individual's needs are satisfied before higher levels can be met, and suggests that emotions reflect the level of satisfaction which an individual experiences. These levels are dynamic, and are dependent upon the individual's capacity to meet the safety, psychological and self-actualisation needs. This self-actualisation means the full development of a child's capabilities and talents. It is essential to have a child's physiological needs met first, and unfortunately in the world, there are too many children wallowing at the base of the pyramid. Secondly, there is a need to feel that the world is organised and predictable and a child feels safe, secure and stable within that basic need. Thirdly, a child needs to have some self-esteem, as well as the esteem of other people. This means to achieve the best of which they are able, to be competent and independent and to have a need for recognition and respect from others. All children need to feel secure, loved and to have the opportunity to love others. When these basic needs are met, motivation will direct behaviour towards fulfilling the higher level needs, which means the needs to live up to one's fullest and unique potential, to know and understand, and the needs for beauty and order and, finally, self-actualisation.

From these basic human needs, both parents and teachers will note that gifted and talented children will need to learn skills to develop their effective base before the acquisition of competent skills can occur, and they need to integrate their skills to meet the fundamental needs of their children.

In the same way, Rimm's Hierarchy of Cognitive Needs (1989) states that the 3Rs, to which the writer would add environment, sit at the base of the hierarchy of intellectual needs. These basic skills are pre-requisite to the middle levels of the hierarchy, knowledge and its applications, and the analysis, synthesis and evaluation of ideas which, in turn, are required for the top level of the hierarchy, creative production. All gifted and talented children should be encouraged to move towards higher levels of the hierarchy. However, they cannot achieve the higher growth levels if they have not mastered the deficiency level of basic skills. If the deficiency needs are not met, the gifted child is likely to perform as a gifted child with average, or below average abilities, and therefore, will not be identified as gifted. From what has been discussed so far, readers will see that they have a vital role because all of us have to look at the whole child.

**The early crucial years**

One of the ways to help our ablest, very young children, is to admit them to school earlier than is normal and indeed, most children now have the opportunity to go to school in England soon after the age of four, and this has been well supported by research (Reynolds *et al.*, 1976; Proctor *et al.*, 1986). While these studies have varied in their criteria for selecting students and in their methods for ascertaining success, the general conclusions have consistently been in favour of early admission to school. It is, however, important that these children are well screened before being admitted and some teachers are very cautious, in that early entry into school may cause personal, as well as academic and social problems. This is where parents and teachers should work closely together and look at some of the variables before making the decision. The following are some other points that should be carefully considered.

*Reading readiness*

This is a skill which is most crucial to early school success and, of course, many gifted children are able to read prior to school entrance.

*Gender*

We have to remember that males do mature later and that it is often young girls who are more physically mature and, therefore, are ready to go to school earlier than boys.

*Eye/hand co-ordination*

Children admitted earlier should have reasonable motor skills, otherwise this could put unnecessary stress on a young child who is unable to draw, cut materials and write.

*Health*

The early years are a time for common ailments to be caught by children and the child who has a history of good health is more likely to attend school regularly and be able to concentrate.

*Social, emotional and physical maturity*

This is largely the decision of the parent, in consultation with the teacher, because it is essential that the child is really ready to appreciate and gain from going to school early. This means the support of the family that values education (please see the section on acceleration).

Many parents are sensitive observers of their own children and know when their children have special talents. This is where parents can inform teachers that their youngsters have unique abilities, and a joint evaluation can then take place (please see parent nomination form).

Teachers may be able to help parents by discussing the following:

(1)  Is your child curious about the world and keen on exploring and discovering its meaning?

(2)  Is your child interested in the whys and the wheres, as well as the hows and the whys, as well as always asking questions?

(3)  Is your child really well above the age level and is possibly even self-taught?

(4)  Does the child have a good vocabulary?

(5)  Did your child start to walk and talk earlier than average?

(6)  Does your child show special abilities in such areas as problem-solving, art, music and even mathematics?

(7)  Does your child appear to be unusually attentive and able to concentrate?

(8)  Does your child show advanced motor skills and is your child good at physical activities?

An honest discussion of these characteristics would be most helpful in identifying gifted and talented children and in coming to a decision as to early admission to school.

To find out whether your child has gifts and talents is one thing, but we have to remember this is a continuing process, because your child's needs, interests and behaviour change with time. Also, a child's growth and development is uneven, and therefore, continuous assessment and recording of behaviour in discussion with the school is very important. Likewise, children make sense of their world by using their senses and should be given every opportunity to expose them to a variety of experiences. For example, your child needs the experience of playing the piano to show outstanding talent in that field. The more opportunities your child has to take part in a wide range of activities, the more likely it will be that his or her gifts and talents will be detected. This is not to say that you should be rigid, but be flexible in the use of time to accommodate interests and encourage perseverance.

We now know that the environment begins to exert an influence on the child before birth and that a favourable pre-birth environment will enhance intellectual growth and development. Young children are unique genetically and their IQ has a strong inherited base, but that intelligence is manifold and more than the narrow quality measured by IQ tests. We also now know that they need optimum environments to maximise their potential, and that other domains, other than the cognitive, must be considered in our search for the early precursors of giftedness, and should not be studied apart from the environmental factors. Education in the early years in general has long practised individual learning by the children, creating a unique environment for each child and ideally, this should carry through to the secondary phase of education, although it is harder here because of the needs of the individual and the demands of society for a flow of trained manpower. There is some incompatibility between an individual's needs and those of society, as witnessed by the controversial debate in education at the present time, but basically, as indicated earlier, individual learning is sound both educationally and biologically.

The concept of gifted infants is unwarranted and the reality is probably that during this period, there is only potential for giftedness that requires an optimum environment for full development.

Burton White (White *et al.*, 1979) described the work of his Harvard project, in which he studied the development of several hundred children over some twelve years. In these studies, it was found that the average Western environment can be expected to contain all that it needed for the development of most human abilities during the first few months of life, and that there is evidence that the rate of achievement of abilities in these first months can be substantially increased. In addition, children can learn to use their hands as reaching tools by three and a half months, rather than by five. Breirley (1978) states that at the age of five, the brain has reached 95 per cent of its adult weight and by this time, he suggests that half of the intellectual growth of a child is complete.

The Harvard project discovered that by the end of the second year of life, an infant has gained two-thirds to three-quarters of all the language she will ever use in ordinary conversation for the rest of her life, including all the major grammatical elements in her native language and a receptive vocabulary of about a thousand words. In addition, an infant at this age will have developed thinking skills, most of the attitudes towards learning and a full range of social skills.

Parents, who are the most important teachers that a child ever has, should be aware of this rapid development of intelligence during the early years, as well as the crucial development stages, and that a child craves experience.

The brain has a timetable of development altered by experience. For instance, a child is able at about the age of three to start searching systematically for experiences and therefore, children at play is a serious business. It is about work learning, not about relaxation. With this in mind, play is sophisticated and toys need to look and sound as real as possible. For example, a graded abacus and a toy telephone. This is also why pre-school education has lasting benefits and a diversity of provision will reap many rewards in terms of the quality of life of a child into adulthood.

The effects of early nutrition on the brain's mature capabilities are crucial. Poor nutrition in pregnancy may not be so important as nutrition in the first two or three years of life, because the mother's foetus may be protected from poor nutrition, but by the end of the first two years of life, the growth spurt of the brain is over. Relatively lethargic children may be so for reasons of poor diet and late nights, they can be less stimulated and not develop well. We need to take note of the evidence of crucial periods of any child's learning. Flexibility of mind, an exceptional immaturity at birth compared with other animals, gives humans a unique capacity for development. Interaction with a stimulating environment, including language, is critical to the mind's development. The brain contains a model of the world built up through the senses. The model creating the brain cells depends on the quality of experience a child has.

Each of us has different models and information fed into the brain through the senses is scanned against the model and decisions taken as a result of the scanning process. A child needs to explore, talk and play with others to refine the model and the quality of the environment influences the model. If deprived, then a poor state of mind is created which learns to expect little out of life. Evidence suggests that memory is stored rather diffusely within the brain tissue and cognitive development is a reflection of interest and maturation, as well as biological and inherited ability.

In this age of computers and space travel, our understanding of our own mind is only just beginning, and much more research is needed. Scientific evidence now indicates that only the left half of our brain is capable of expressing its thoughts in words fully, and the right side of the brain has its own separate train of thoughts, which are not in words. Though these non-verbal thoughts are a crucial part of our personality and abilities, they continue to be ignored and misunderstood because they are so difficult to translate into words. Since the right side of the brain is capable of controlling our actions, remembering things, solving problems and having our emotional selves developed, it fully qualifies as a mind by itself. Inspite of this fact, we have continued to look at our mind as a single entity that thinks only in words. When you look at a human brain, it is difficult to see how anyone could ever have thought of it as the physical basis of a single mind, for the human brain is obviously a double organ consisting of two identical looking hemispheres joined together by bundles of nerve fibres called the Corpus callosum. Certainly the billions of neurons in the two hemispheres are not so identical that they can simultaneously conceive identical thoughts on each side, yet the human mind resides strictly in one of the hemispheres. What could the equal amount of brainpower in the other hemisphere be doing? Most of the organs of the body are in pairs and evolutionary forces simply do not allow the kind of waste that would be represented by having one hemisphere sit idle. In fact, measurements of the rate of metabolism of the two hemispheres indicates that both are doing the same amount of work.

Contemporary understanding of human brain functions establishes that each side of the brain is unique and that brains in general are specialised. While experts argue about the degree of specialisation (Herrmann, 1987), there is a general agreement on the fact of specialisation. For example, there is agreement on the concept of dominance; eye dominance, hand dominance, foot dominance, ear dominance and brain dominance. While the body is symmetrical in terms of organ duality, that is we have two eyes, two ears, two hands, two feet and two hemispheres, in the use of these dual organs, there exists a general asymmetry. In other words, we use one to a greater degree than the other. When combined, the concepts of specialisation and asymmetry, or dominance, produce within each human being a distribution of specialised preferences that affect general behaviour. Specifically included is a unique individual's learning style. This has important implications for both parents and teachers of children, in that intelligence is no longer one-dimensional, but rather includes the notion of multiple intelligences (see table 5.1).

Each individual is a unique learner with learning preferences and avoidances different from other learners.

All this points to the need to provide optimum conditions for all children from birth and we should not be satisfied until all children are born into homes where parents have the knowledge and skills to meet all the needs of the growing child and are sufficiently affluent to do so. Experiences that a child has in the early primary years seem to matter for the rest of life, because of the physical changes in the cortex, which are perhaps unchangeable, but deprivation cannot be solved by schools alone. The influence of the streets, television, homes and youth organisations, to give a few examples, are crucial. Parent/school liaison is of the greatest importance and a difficult art. The school should not undermine the dignity and authority of the parents with the children. Perhaps of the early years 0–5 are the most crucial; then the brain is undergoing maximum growth and is probably at its most plastic. This is when the quality of the environment can be crucial. To give one further example, the brain is built to mop up language incredibly quickly. Babies are born with the left (language) hemisphere larger than the right. Therefore, language, like food, is a basic need, and it is essential that children are talked to and not treated to 'shut-up' answers.

## Which schools will provide the best education for my child?

There is no easy answer to this question but the following list of what makes an effective school can assist parents when making choices:

### 1. Qualities of pupils
A mixture of backgrounds or abilities seems to be best, although the key appears to be to have a large enough concentration of pupils who come to school with good academic skills. Too great a concentration of children with poor skills makes it more difficult for the rest of the things on this list to occur.

### 2. Goals of the school
A strong emphasis on excellence with high standards in both academic and non-academic areas and high expectations, characterises effective schools. These goals are clearly stated by the administration and shared by all the staff.

### 3. Organisation of classrooms
It seems that daily activities need to be structured with a high percentage of time spent in actually group teaching (as opposed to planning and organising for instruction or in behaviour management). High expectations of perform-

ance are conveyed to all pupils. There should be provision of a variety of curriculum options for gifted talents to be identified and encouraged.

### 4. *Praise*
High praise for good performance, for meeting expectations, for really trying, are given to pupils. These are structured but warm schools. (See Maslow's hierarchy of needs.)

### 5. *Homework*
Homework is assigned regularly and marked quickly. Effective schools assign markedly more homework than do less effective schools.

### 6. *Discipline*
Most discipline is handled within the classroom, with readily little fallback to sending children to the head teacher. But in really effective schools, not much class time is actually spent in discipline because these teachers have very good control of the class. They intervene early with a potentially difficult situation rather than imposing heavy discipline after the fact.

### 7. *Teacher experience*
Teacher education is not necessarily related to the effectiveness of schools, but teacher experience is, presumably because it takes time to learn effective class management and teaching strategies. It probably also takes specific guidance and training from experienced teachers to help in this learning process. The importance of mentors for probationary teachers cannot be stressed too much.

The staff should believe that education of children is the joint responsibility of both staff and parents and encourage community involvement wherever possible.

### 8. *Resources*
The school should have sufficient facilities, resources and staff to be flexible in its organisation and the staff should be aware of and sensitive to the needs of all children.

### 9. *Surroundings*
Age or general appearance of the school building is not critical, but maintenance in good order, cleanliness, and attractiveness do appear to matter. School ethos starts with the receptionist and the appearance of the entrance.

### 10. *School leadership*
Clear values, shared and readily stated by school senior staff, are a major key. The academic emphasis of the school must be apparent in all school activities, in allocation of funds, in priorities of time usage.

### 11. *Responsibilities for children*
In effective schools, children are more likely to be given real responsibilities in individual classrooms and in school as a whole.

The children should be actively involved in their own learning and given the opportunity to show their talents.

### 12. *The whole child*
The school should develop the whole child; body, mind and spirit and should show a concern for the cultural and social backgrounds of children.

### Helping children at home

(1)  They are still children. They need love, but controls; attention but discipline; parental involvement, yet training in self-dependence and responsibility.

(2)  Often the gifted child feels isolated from the rest of the world because of the exceptional abilities he or she possesses. Facing these feelings of difference alone can create emotional problems, disruptive behaviours, or withdrawal from the frustrating situation.

(3)  Consonance of parental value systems is important for their optimum development. This means that there should not be wide disagreements over values between parents.

(4)  Parental involvement in early task demands, such as training them to perform tasks themselves, to count, tell time, use correct vocabulary and pronunciation, locate themselves and get around their neighbourhood, do errands and be responsible are all important.

(5)  Emphasis on early verbal expression, reading, discussing ideas in the presence of children, poetry and music are all valuable. Parents should read to children. There should be an emphasis by parents on doing well in school.

(6)  Encourage children to play with words. Even in such common settings as a car ride or shopping trip, word games, like rhyming, opposites and puns can be used to their full advantage.

(7)  Provide a variety of books, magazines, puzzles, and games which promote use of the imagination, logical thinking, drawing inferences and making predictions.

(8)  Help gifted and talented individuals become critical viewers and readers by discussing influences, the mass media such as television and literature may have personal and social values.

(9)  The lack of disruption of family life through divorce or separation, and the maintenance of a happy, healthy home is an important aspect in raising able children, as well as other children.

(10)  Since able children often have vague awareness of adult problems such as sex, death, sickness, finances, war, etc. which their lack of experience makes them unable to solve, they may need reassurance in these areas.

(11)  Encourage children to play an active, real role in family decisions. Listen to their suggestions, applying them wherever possible. For example, when planning a trip or vacation, have gifted children participate in decisions about places, routes, food and activities. Respect their suggestions, and assign important tasks appropriate to their abilities – such as map reader on a trip or bookkeeper of the family budget.

(12)  Explore ways of finding and solving problems by asking questions, posing hypotheses, discussing alternative solutions and evaluating

those alternatives. Personal and family situations may be used, as well as the larger social issues of the town, the country or the world.

(13) Help the child relate to friends who may not be so gifted. While gifted children should recognise their abilities, they should also learn to put them into perspective with the abilities and interests of others. Instead of setting themselves above others, they should learn to look for strengths in friends as well as for ways to share their abilities in a productive manner.

(14) The role of good books, magazines and other aids to home learning, such as encyclopaedias, charts, collections, are important.

(15) Parents should take the initiative in taking able children to museums, art galleries, educational institutions and other historical places where collections of various sorts may enhance background learning.

(16) Parents should be especially careful not to 'shut up' the gifted child who asks questions. In particular, he should not be scolded for asking, nor should it be inferred that this is an improper or forbidden subject. The parent may, however, insist that questions not be asked at inappropriate times, and he may require the child to sharpen or re-phrase his question so as to clarify it. Sometimes questions should not be answered completely, but the reply should itself be a question which sends the child into some larger direction. When the parent cannot answer the questions, he should direct the child to a resource which can.

(17) There's a difference between pushing and intellectual stimulation. Parents should avoid 'pushing' a child into reading, 'exhibiting' him before others or courting undue publicity about him. On the other hand, parents should seek in every way to stimulate and widen the child's mind, through suitable experiences in books, recreation, travel and the arts.

(18) Prize and praise efforts and accomplishments. Support children when they succeed as well as when they don't succeed. Create an atmosphere where risk taking is OK.

(19) Encourage the gifted and talented to challenge themselves. Because of their superior abilities, the gifted often work at only partial capacity in various areas and still succeed. This approach to learning, however, may ultimately create difficulties because the individuals may acquire extremely poor learning habits which they may not be able to over-come when they are sufficiently challenged.

## Stimulating activities to do with your children at home

(1) Play Scrabble 'ad lib' using only words around a theme. For example, farm, Christmas, weather. Children must give rationale for words used.

(2)   Pick a household item and invent 10 new uses for it apart from the obvious. Design the perfect broom, vacuum cleaner or sink.

(3)   Listen to a foreign radio station. Pick up a foreign newspaper and explore it with the child; listen to the music. Borrow records from the library. Plan a dish from that country and then create your own, using products similar to the native recipes. This is a good introduction to global education.

(4)   Plan a trip and mention problems that arise. Let the children solve the problem with yellow pages, newspapers and maps.

(5)   Write letters to manufacturers praising or complaining about their products. Make suggestions for improvement. Include a catchy commercial jingle. Discuss commercials for obvious and hidden messages. Enter a manufacturer's contest.

(6)   Invite an elderly member of the family to discuss old times and life 50 years ago. Design a family crest or flag depicting family history and symbols of family's value system. Prepare a motto to accompany the crest. Work out a family tree. Keep a diary of family or personal events and make each entry different, such as a poem, slogan, illustration, song lyrics.

(7)   Investigate various forms of communication in your home, body language, facial expressions, conversation, animal communication, media. Design your own code of communication.

(8)   Chart the routine of animals and plan a change in habits. Record the changes in behaviour in the development of a habit. Design the perfect fictitious household pet, borrowing characteristics of other animals.

(9)   Have the child redesign his bedroom to accommodate his hobbies and interests. Allow suggestions for architectural and structural changes on paper. Have the child find a new way to make a bed, decorate a window or set a table. Have the child give the rationale for his changes.

(10)  Listen to a different kind of music such as jazz, calypso, swing, as well as classical. Discuss mood and interpretation of music and encourage free dance expression to the music. Rent or borrow an instrument and investigate musical patterns.

(11)  Discuss a favourite TV programme and plan two plots and sub-plots for the characters. Relate characteristics of characters to friends and relatives. Discuss plausibility of the present plots and relate them to their own personal experiences.

(12)  Star gaze and investigate astronomy. Learn about calendars to which other different cultures adhere (Hebrew, Chinese). Create a new month with a new holiday. Children are fascinated by the sky at night.

(13)  Watch a new sport. Play your own invented sport and logical rules, uniforms and equipment.

(14)  Scour the newspapers for local problems and plan logical solutions.

Write letters to the Editor.
(15) Learn a new craft.
(16) Ask the child to condense a film, book or TV programme to four sentences or four words.
(17) Create and illustrate a cartoon strip featuring original animated characters or hero.
(18) Devise a weather station for recording conditions and predictions. Plan novel ways of conserving energy and water based on your findings.
(19) Devise a new maths value system and plan equations in your system. Explore unfamiliar operations on a calculator.
(20) Learn about perennial and annual plants and plan a timetable for flowering.
(21) Plan a simple chemical experiment from household items. Explore chemical components of household items and food stuffs. Discuss chemical changes in food and additives.
(22) Solve crossword puzzles or anagrams and construct your own. Plan riddles and pantomimes.
(23) Explore infrequently visited spots in your home for 'antiques'. Critique the value of items. Discuss economic concepts such as appreciation/depreciation. Have the children plan a car boot sale and evaluate the items for sale.
(24) Read current world news items. Analyse the articles for solutions and discuss how the possible solutions will filter down to affect their lives.

## Look at the whole child

This book has somewhat followed the traditional model of defining who we are talking about, identifying the children and providing a special programme. It also suggests a new model which should have as its basis the provision of a rich, stimulating experience which extends all children to the highest potential of which they are capable in a climate which fosters creativity and allows some freedom of choice. As gifted behaviour is observed to emerge under these conditions, the sensitive teachers and school, as well as the parental support, will provide opportunities of further development.

The tendency in education, and this will probably increase, is to develop the cognitive areas of a child to the detriment of the cultural, physical and the spiritual dimensions. For example, there is a growing interest in the idea that we can all take more responsibility for our own health and a recognition of good health is more than freedom from disease or infirmity. The idea of a holistic living programme is now the fastest growing and most important development in the domain of health and healing. It is a programme of self-care in which a person is seen as a whole – body, mind and spirit and the parts interrelated. Despite the tendency in schools for physical education to decline, it is essential to develop a healthy mind and healthy body.

From whatever point of view one contemplates the educational scene, one sees at once a marked division between the mind and the spirit. Certain things are not quantifiable and with the emphasis on cost effectiveness and efficiency, we have to guard against the decline in the quality of life as a whole. The mind has to do with the ability to deduce cause and effect, to follow a logical argument, to reason, to calculate, to memorise facts, to infer and deduce. It is these attributes of man more than any others which have enabled us to make Concorde, but also the nuclear bomb. Our spirit is different. It has to do with fears and joys, enthusiasms and apathies, loves and hates. It is this side of our nature which more than our minds decides when we shall release the bomb and whom we should kill with it. It accounts for the emotional mess in Northern Ireland as well as the compassion of Oxfam. It accounts for the driving force of men like Gandhi and the whole army of creative people. The differences between mind and spirit show themselves in simpler ways which are within our grasp in an average class-room. There is, for example, a difference between the mechanical process of reading and the enjoyment of what is read; between the mechanics of musical notation and sensitive playing and singing; between writing on a prescribed topic from notes on a blackboard and telling someone in your own personal written words something that has excited you; between lessons on perspective and giving a child the urge to draw or paint; it is the difference between the teacher who tries to find out why the child is ill-behaved and remove the cause, and the teacher who obtains a purely superficial result by sarcasm; between the teacher who ranks and grades children solely on their achievements and the one that makes allowances for handicaps and judges effort; between the head of a school who sees the timetable and the framing of school rules as his main task and the one who, by the use of recognition, expectation and encouragement, draws the best out of both colleagues and pupils.

Now of course one cannot divide the curriculum into the things of the mind and things of the spirit. Indeed, we talked earlier about the holistic approach to a child's education. If a child is good at arithmetic but loathes it, the failure in my terms is one of the spirit. But it is a fact that in our education system, we tend to attach more importance to things of the mind that can be measured, to subjects which traffic in these things to the teachers who can teach them and to the children who are good at them, than we do to other activities which deal mainly with the spirit and whose manifest-ations defy measurement.

Parents have an essential role to develop the whole child and to encourage health and religious education. This neglected affective area of education, which in addition to developing spirituality includes self-concepts, self-esteem, values and moral thinking, social adjustments, altruism and motivation, is essential for the development of well-rounded, fulfilled and outgoing students. In an earlier checklist, we discussed the fact that most gifted and talented children are well able to understand moral issues and the ability to discuss them as well as being basically honest, ethical and truthful. The home has a vital role to play here because teachers are under considerable pressure with large classes, testing and the National Curriculum to implement. The school should look at all the positive attributes of a child and tell each child of their capabilities and worthwhileness. Developing a good self-concept is a goal of every school and is a motivating force to give children higher aspirations and achievements. There are many perceptions of self including:

- Body Self – which includes understanding changes and the use and misuse of the body.
- Sexual Self – understanding sexual development and the role of sexuality in relationships.
- Vocational Self – making contributions to society, lifestyles and developing awareness.
- Social Self – understanding others' perspectives, their role in relationships, coping with conflicts, working with others and making sense of others.
- Moral Self – the making of judgements, resolving moral dilemmas, taking action on issues.
- Self as a learner – understanding strengths and weaknesses and reflecting on approaches to learning.
- Self – the organisation – becoming an active member of the school, giving and gaining benefits.

Given time, commitment and opportunities, schools can teach a humanistic, caring curriculum which includes exposing children to problems of the elderly and handicapped, involvement in community service, raising money for worthwhile projects, recycling materials in school which raises awareness of environmental issues, to debates about pollution, over population, AIDS, abortion and other current issues of real concern.

Table 6.1

| Body | Mind | Spirit | Relationship | Environment |
|---|---|---|---|---|
| Exercise | Thought | Beliefs | Family | Soil |
| Food | Feelings | Values | Friends | Plants |
| Illness | Ideas | Experience | Community | Animals |
| Health | | Faith | Society | Weather |
| | | | | Water |
| | | | | Air |

The writer is hoping to write individualised learning kits which will enrich the curriculum in some of these areas discussed and this would be the basis of a holistic curriculum over and above that provided by the National Curriculum: see Table 6.1

This is a fundamental area of concern if we are to have a caring society and one in which parents can contribute so much at home, but also in schools. These five areas will make a genuine, enriching curriculum.

# CHAPTER 7

# *Resources and Policies*

> Do not then, train youth to learn by force and harshness, but lead them to it by what amuses their minds so that they may discover the peculiar bent of the genius of each. (Plato)

> Never mistake knowledge for wisdom. One helps you make a living: the other helps you make a life. (Sandra Carey)

Until recently, education in Britain has been dominated by two key concepts – those of growth and equality. This situation is now changing and our emphasis must switch to a sustained concern for the quality of the enterprise.

With the demise of the Schools Council Gifted Children Project, the National Association for Curriculum Enrichment and Extension was established with a basic aim to help teachers particularly to turn potential into performance by enriching and extending the curriculum for our more able children in schools. This work now continues in conjunction with the National Association for Gifted Children.

NACE challenges the contemporary viewpoint that quality can be obtained by standardising the curriculum, concentrating on the so-called 'basic skills' and developing new systems, monitoring and assessment – moves which inevitably lead to greater centralised control of schools and the curriculum. Quality requires the full recognition of individual differences and the wide range of society's needs. Quality in education must relate to quality of life itself and cannot be achieved without opportunities for specialism and individual enrichment. In the end the achievement of quality must depend on the skills of the teaching profession and the co-operation received from both parents and the community as a whole.

There is a tendency today to equate the needs of industry with that of education and to use industry as a model for the educational system. It is possibly true that certain procedures from industry can be adopted to improve quality in education. Two in particular stand out: firstly, we can work on the design of products to make them more useful, efficient or long-lasting; secondly, we can seek to modify the production techniques in order to create better quality output in relation to cost. Both factors can also be applied to education. We can seek to improve educational quality first by modifying the objectives and goals of the end product and secondly, by working on the techniques, processes and structures of the enterprise so that the desirable objectives can be more clearly achieved. It is, however, also important to recognise that whilst we can draw industrial parallels of this kind, there are crucial differences as well. Firstly, pupils are not raw material to be moulded into any shape that educational designers consider appropriate. Each child is a unique individual with tremendous potential, having wishes and wills of their own which must be taken into full consideration. Any decisions as to what should be taught and to which pupils, how much learning should be structured and presented, must take account of the fact that pupils are persons in their own right – individual centres of consciousness, feeling and will. As long as teachers and parents recognise this and give individual children time, then the National Curriculum can be of great benefit to all children. Secondly, pupils, unlike raw materials in factories, do not spend all their time in one place. What they do at home and elsewhere, their leisure activities, the TV programmes they watch, the various people they meet and talk with, have just as profound an influence on the quality of their education as formal schooling. Hence a concern for educational quality cannot simply be left as an objective for teachers and administrators. It must be the concern of the whole community.

One of the objectives of NACE and others, therefore, has been to produce resources to assist teachers concerned about helping the more able children to reach their potential. If the average class teacher is to be able to give the most effective help to all children in her care, then it follows that she needs all the support that it is possible to provide. Many pupils are learning efficiently and are developing their individual talents. However, there is concern that some of our more able children are underachieving and I do hope this guide will be helpful to enrich and extend the curriculum for these children. The task, therefore, is not to rescue an enterprise that has collapsed, or is in danger of doing so, but to build up an enterprise to achieve even more significant degrees of achievement, to make sure we are working along the right lines for the good of all our children.

There follow some useful addresses for recommended materials purporting to be differentiated and to be genuine enrichment over and above the content of the National Curriculum. However, few have been vigorously evaluated and this is a challenge.

**Centre for Creativity, Innovation and Leadership** – materials mainly about innovative thinking and leadership are available from the Associate Director, Hilda Rosselli, Human Sciences Building 414, University of Florida, Tampa, FL 33620, USA.

**The DES Library Bibliography 39 Gifted Children** – contains books and articles. A free copy can be obtained from the Department of Education and Science, London.

**Dorset, Direct Education Supplies** – includes teacher's manual and 31 activity packs.

**Essex Curriculum Extension Projects** – available from Dr. Julian Whybra.

**European Council for High Ability** – has an excellent journal, newsletters, holds conferences and undertakes research.

**Exceptionality Education, Canada** – a new journal edited by Judy Luport of the University of Calgary to encourage scholarly exchange of ideas.

**Gifted Education International** is a useful journal edited by Belle Wallace and published by AB Academic Publishers, Bicester, Oxon, U.K.

**Hampshire** – has produced valuable Material for the Able Child, MACH, and also, as part of their Curriculum Differentiation Initiative, the publication 'Matching the Curriculum to the Needs of the Individual'.

**The Mathematical Association** – 295 London Road, Leicester LE2 3BE.

**National Association for Curriculum Enrichment and Extension (NACE)** – the aim of the association: 'Able and talented children's lives can be enriched and their thinking skills extended through stimulating learning activities which can be enjoyed by all children'. NACE seeks to achieve this by:

- Encouraging the provision of an enabling climate for learning within the classroom in order to create opportunities for special abilities to manifest themselves and be recognised.
- Supporting those who have a professional concern for the education of able and talented children through a termly newsletter.
- Disseminating good practice through an annual conference and other activities.
- Promoting the education, training and professional development of teachers.
- Seeking to secure appropriate resources for enrichment and extension activities in schools.
- Encouraging the study of able and talented children.
- Liaising with the DES, LEAs and any other organisation engaged in further similar aims to this association.

NACE is based at Nene College, Moulton Park, Northampton NN2 7AL, Tel: (0604) 710308.

**The National Council for Educational Technology (NCET)** – Sir W. Lyons Road, Science Park, University of Warwick, Coventry CV4 7EZ, encourages supported self-study and has a consultancy and an information service.

**The National Association for Gifted Children (NAGC)** – this is an association of parents, teachers and other adults interested in the development and education of gifted children. It was founded in 1966 and helps parents and children through its ever-growing number of branches all over the UK. Membership categories include family, individual, student and corporate. Publications include: newsletters, help with bright children and counselling. Further information can be obtained from the National Centre for Able and Talented Children, Nene College, Moulton Park Campus, Northampton NN2 7AL. (NACE and NAGC now have joint Headquarters at Nene College.)

**Nene Publications** – have enrichment kits on Advertising; the Latin Connection – the development of the English language; Tudor England; Slugs and Snails; Woodlice. These publications can be obtained from the author, Nene College, Moulton Park, Northampton NN2 7AL.

**Newcastle Materials for the More Able 5–7 Years** – Jim Standish, Gosforth Park First School, Newcastle-upon-Tyne.

**Odyssey of the Mind** – Mastery Education Corporation, 85 Main Street, Waterwon MA 02172, USA.

**Philosophy for Children**, Institute for the Advancement of Philosophy for Children, Montclair State College, Upper Montclair, NJ 07043, USA.

**The Potential Trust and Questors** – the aim of the Trust:

> To help children with special needs, whose needs arise from a high degree of unfulfilled potential in one or more areas – intellectual, practical, aesthetic, creative, social, personal – by complementing the provision already made for such children by parents and schools, in co-operation with other individuals and organisations working in the same field.

The Trust runs interesting holidays for able children and their address is Shepherds Close, Kingston Stert, Chinnor, Oxon OX9 4NL.

**Pullen Publications Limited** – 121 London Road, Knebworth, Herts SG3 6EX, produce enrichment and extension material.

**Queensland Association for Gifted and Talented Children** – P.O. Box 121 Ashgrove, QLD 4060, Australia. Queensland is the only state in Australia which has a full team of some eight or nine inspectors concentrating upon curriculum extension and enrichment for the talented and able.

**Reach** – is the Solihull Metropolitan Borough Council's Resource Centre and has probably best reference collection of enrichment resources in Britain.

**Schools Council Gifted Children Programme** – four publications from Longman.

**Shell Education Service** – Shell UK Limited, Shell Mex House, Strand, London WC2R 0DX have produced a number of study projects related to industry, science and technology and these are available from Bankside House, West Mills, Newbury, Berks RG14 5HP.

**Talented** is a recommended newsletter which includes ideas and resources and is available from UNE Armidale, CB Newling Centre, Armidale, NSW, Australia.

**Trillium Press** – a major American publisher who specialises in enrichment and extension publications and materials, P.O. Box 209, Monroe, NY 10950, USA.

**World Council for Gifted and Talented Children** – biennial proceedings from World Conferences on the resources available from Trillium Press, P.O. Box 209, Monroe, NY 10950, USA. Has developed an international diploma for teachers of gifted and talented children. The World conferences provide a world forum for research, materials and the exchange of ideas.

Readable and helpful books for teachers will be found in the Bibliography, see especially: Bloom, Clarke, Denton, Davis and Rimm, Eyre and Marjoram, Feldhusen, Freeman, Gallagher, Leyden, Maltby, Ogilvie, Postlethwaite and Denton, Renzulli, Sternberg, Tear and Wallace.

In order to offer an effective service in meeting the needs of gifted and talented children in schools, governors, parents, teachers and other involved professionals need to be clear about what school policies exist in general, but what policy there is, in particular, for these children. Policies should form part of the overall curriculum plan for the school. The gifted and talented children should be educated in a way which enables them to work at the highest level, both for the good of others and for their own satisfaction. It is generally recognised that those of exceptional high ability, in whatever area of human endeavour, require rich, challenging experiences to achieve some fulfillment.

Schools should have clear policies concerning the needs of pupils, which includes ways of identifying them and monitoring their progress, as well as making provision that is consonant with the National Curriculum, but which also enriches and extends it. It should make clear what strategies it will follow in the case of a child displaying general giftedness across the curriculum, or specific talents in any aspect of the child's work. This will mean addressing such issues as acceleration, enrichment and extension of the curriculum, and such developments should take place on a whole-school basis, taking into account those children who are far more able than their peers, as well as the generally accepted 10 per cent who would be identified nationally as more able.

In devising this policy concerning the needs of our gifted and talented children, one should expect to see:

# Questionnaire on departmental provision for more able pupils

Please answer the following questions by ticking the appropriate box or boxes.

1. Do you have any 'more able' pupils in your department/class?

| YES | NO | DON'T KNOW |
|---|---|---|
| | | |

2. Which procedures do you use, if any, to identify able pupils?

| TESTS | PROGRESS REPORTS | TEACHER ASSESSMENT | PARENT REPORTS | NONE |
|---|---|---|---|---|
| | | | | |

3. What provision, if any, do you make for able pupils?

| WITHDRAWAL GROUPS | ENRICHMENT MATERIAL | ACCELERATION | OTHER | NONE |
|---|---|---|---|---|
| | | | | |

4. Are there any specific difficulties in providing for able pupils in your department/class?

| LARGE CLASSES | STAFF SHORTAGE | LACK OF RESOURCES | OTHER | NONE |
|---|---|---|---|---|
| | | | | |

5. Do you make additional arrangements to accommodate the more able pupils?

| CLUBS | PARENTAL INVOLVEMENT | AFTER SCHOOL ACTIVITIES | EDUCATIONAL VISITS | NONE |
|---|---|---|---|---|
| | | | | |

6. Do you have special resources for the more able child?

| YES | NO | DON'T KNOW |
|---|---|---|
| | | |

7. Is there anyone responsible for able children in your department?

| YES | NO |
|---|---|
| | |

(1) Consistent terminology and definition. For Britain, where a National Curriculum has recently been implemented, then a definition might well be as follows:

Gifted and talented students are those students whose functioning is at least at the upper end or above that normally associated with that key stage and whose abilities are so well-developed or so far in advance of their peer group, that a school has to provide additional learning experiences which develop, enhance and extend the identified abilities. This definition should then be accompanied by a profile of the child which will assist the teacher to consider the first stage of identification. The school then needs to consider – have we any children like this? How are we meeting their needs?

(2) Senior management should then define and agree methods for screening, registering and monitoring the progress of pupils with these abilities.

(3) To provide advice on identifying gifted and talented children.

(4) Aims and objectives should be set which reflect the idea that the provision for able children should be seen as an aspect of provision for all pupils. Therefore, it is important to raise the awareness of all staff, and that management provide training and guidance to enable all teachers to meet the needs of these children.

(5) As staff agreement is reached on the appropriate procedures for recognition, provision and assessment of children, then it is important that each member of staff has a sense of ownership.

(6) Teachers should provide opportunities for pupils to practise and develop their particular abilities, that the children who share these abilities are provided with opportunities to get together to share and develop their talents, and this can be provided in a variety of ways.

(7) To build up a directory of useful local expertise which may assist these children in their work, including the appointment of mentors.

(8) These pupils should work, for the most part, with their peers in ways that lead to social and emotional maturity and which help them to build strong relationships with others.

(9) To develop a collection of appropriate resources.

(10) To keep records about and monitor the progress of the children identified.

### The role of the school co-ordinator

Once a policy has been agreed, it is essential to have a school co-ordinator appointed, and such a person needs highly-developed perception and communication skills. In many schools, such a role befalls the Special Education Needs co-ordinator, who has more than enough to do and a case needs to be made for the children we are discussing here who also have special needs. Such a co-ordinator would have the following role in the school:

(1) To initiate the formulation and revision of the school policy.

(2) Consultation with the senior management of the school and all the staff.

(3)　To call for nominations from staff, parents and students (please see the form which follows).

(4)　To maintain awareness of parent trends in Britain and abroad, external agencies, dissemination of information to all staff, and to advise on the availability of in-service courses in this area of expertise.

(5)　To identify, invite and match mentors to students and to arrange an initial meeting between students, mentors and parents.

(6)　To organise the expertise of staff and devise a talent pool of advisers and inspectors of the LEA.

(7)　To liaise with parents of our gifted and talented children.

(8)　To initiate and maintain the agreed system of profiling, including testing.

(9)　To establish systems for cross-phase liaison.

(10)　To regularly follow up students' progress with mentors, supervising teachers and students.

(11)　Meeting the needs of these children by using planned educational programmes, tutors from other establishments, targeted resources and the library as a multi-media resource base would solve many National Curriculum issues.

Attainment targets are now age-related in law, creating problems in managing provision for very able pupils. Such pupils may make rapid progress through to a point in the levels beyond their key stage. If schools make provision for such pupils whilst at the same time keeping them with their age group peers, technically the school would be breaking the law. Therefore, in the school policy, there should be a procedure to avoid this, such as advancing the child into the next key stage. This assumes that the pupil will continue to function at an advanced level and would not 'plateau out' in skill or knowledge acquisition and that the pupil can cope socially and emotionally with such acceleration (please see the section on acceleration). Another policy would be to apply to have the National Curriculum dis-applied, although this may or may not be allowed, and would certainly involve the school in an extra burden of administration. The pupil will only carry the equivalent age-related financial weighting, not that of the accelerated key stage. The advice is, however, that because these two options have difficulties, a third option which involves the tutoring model, the provision of extension work. This means the School Policy Group must consider the following questions:

- How can this be planned, managed and delivered?
- How can we extend the way children are involved in their own learning?
- How can children be given even more responsibility for their own learning?
- How can we extend our cross-phase links to encompass tutoring?
- How can the library service help to supplement our resources?
- Have we a targeted plan for resource buying?

# REFERRAL FORM FOR GIFTED, TALENTED OR UNDERACHIEVING CHILDREN

I wish to draw your attention to..................................................................................

in.................................................................................... (Class or Tutor Group)

Please find attached the following:

1. Check list
2. My written description of the child's classroom performance
3. Letter from parent
4. Test results
5. Photocopied evidence from the child's written work
6. Other

Signed ..................................................................................................................

One of the great pleasures of undertaking in-service courses around the country is that schools then implement policy and a plan of action to support teachers and gifted and talented children in schools. This has also meant that a number of schools have sent the author materials of policy in action. The author is grateful for permission to use the following papers from several schools around Britain.

The schools vary from rural to urban; primary to secondary, as well as in approach and level of success to date. They are examples for others to emulate.

### Holyport CE Primary School

This school has a head teacher with a long-standing interest in children with potential. Provision here has grown through a variety of approaches, each one showing the school's developing understanding of the children and issues involved. The emphasis has moved from dealing with individual children to high quality provision for all children – enrichment and extension. The school is situated in a large village with a catchment area of middle class, commuterland parents with above average ability children.

My interest in gifted children goes back to 1971 when I attended a weekend course at our local Teachers' Centre, tutored by Ralph Callow, but it was not until my appointment to my second headship in April 1979 that I had the opportunity to put my thoughts and ideas into practice.

I was able to appoint a Scale 2 postholder with responsibility for curriculum extension for the able child. Like most jobs in the primary school, Deborah had a full-time teaching commitment and worked mainly in an advisory capacity. During the spring and summer of 1980 she and I attended a Regional DES course on able children at Reading University, and this gave us the basis to start work at Holyport. In staff meetings during those two terms, we developed strategies for identifying able children.

- The staff identified the children in their own teams whom they considered able and talented.
- The results from NFER tests of maths, English and verbal reasoning were looked at. These tests are school-administered every year, three weeks into the autumn term. I feel that we get a truer picture of a child's ability in the autumn term than in June/July.
- Any child who had a wide discrepancy in her test results or who appeared on the staff list but not on the test list, or vice versa, had a non-verbal test.
- In a small number of cases where we were still not sure, we discussed the child with parents.
- Finally, in one or two cases, we asked the educational psychologist for an option.

Using the above, we then identified a group of junior-aged children who were talented in the fields of maths and language and these were withdrawn once a week for extension work. This system worked very well for 18 months, although it highlighted a number of advantages and disadvantages. The staff's awareness of children's varying abilities had been heightened and they were beginning to question why we were covering only one facet of the above child categories, mainly high intellect, and then only in maths and English. In their search for 'gold they had found silver' and they now wanted to develop a school policy that would provide for a wide range of gifts and talents. It was decided to tackle this problem in two ways.

Firstly, we extended the resources in the school. This meant allocating money on a regular basis to purchase books, games, workcards, etc. that could be used as extension material. There was, and still is, very little published under this specific heading and, therefore, we had to look at existing publications and suggest alternative ways of using them. This resource bank is now very large and covers all areas of the curriculum. It still has an annual budget in the same way as maths, art or music. It is centralised in the entrance hall of the school and all children are encouraged to use it. Secondly, we decided to set up an activities afternoon each week. The idea was to provide approximately 20 different activities on a termly basis and cover as many interesting experiences as possible, asking the parents if they could offer a talent or hobby that they were prepared to share with the children. We also contacted local advisers: the church groups, the Darby and Joan, in fact, anyone whom we felt could help us! The response was fantastic and for two years we ran an enormous range of experiences for the children – from the usual school subjects of maths and science, to hobbies such as macrame, model-making and cookery, to specialist subjects like astronomy, campanology, architecture and church history.

The postholder for the above children, now a Scale 3, had responsibility for organising the afternoons, Julie arranged that all non-teachers had groups of eight children while teachers had varying groups according to their activity.

Every square inch of the school came into use and children explored the delights of music-making or scientific experiments or gardening. Initially, children were allowed to choose which activity they joined for the team. As the scheme progressed, so children were encouraged to join certain activities to give them a chance to explore their latent talents, often with surprising results.

After two years it was time to reassess the situation. Parents were beginning to help only with the activities afternoon, not with individual children or groups during the rest of the week. Other volunteer help was 'drying up' and the momentum to keep the afternoons interesting and stimulating was becoming more and more difficult.

We were now on to our third postholder. Judith was an infant specialist, and that brought fresh impetus to the staff. It was felt that the children's curriculum development should be catered for within the classroom situation. Each year group works as a team of approximately 60 children with two staff. Each team chooses a termly topic that is brainstormed to include as many aspects of the curriculum as possible. Flow diagrams are prepared to show the development of the topic and assignments written for the different levels of ability. Though the children are initially directed to the assignment suitable for their needs, this does not preclude any child from tackling different levels, often with interesting results.

The problems of writing assignments are then open-ended and challenging. It is not easy; in fact some staff find it very difficult. To help staff, a number of meetings were spent looking at open-ended questioning and the way to write interesting tasks. These sessions threw up the need to look in depth at study skills. Each team write a list of the skills they would expect to teach in a year and these were collected by all staff into a study skills document for 5 to 11 year olds.

In the meanwhile, we had, as a staff, completed writing our policy statements on the curriculum for all the major areas and felt it was time to commit to paper our policy on the able child. As usual a term's staff meetings were devoted to discussion and a paper was eventually produced and submitted to the governors.

### Policy Document for the Able Child
### (Holyport CE Primary School)

*Aims of the school*

'Our main aim is to draw out the special talents and aptitudes of each individual child.'

'To help pupils to develop lively, inquiring minds, the ability to question and argue rationally and to apply themselves to relevant tasks and physical skills.'

'To recognise each child as an individual, to develop self-discipline and help them realise their potential.'

Keeping these aims in mind, provision for the able should be seen as an aspect of provision for all children, as an integral part of equal opportunity for all pupils.

There are several aspects of exceptional ability that need recognition and should be taken into account:

- physical ability
- skill in visual and performing arts
- mechanical ingenuity
- leadership and social awareness
- high intelligence
- creativity (permeating each aspect)

Therefore, the aims of the school for the able child are:

- To appoint a member of staff to lead and co-ordinate work relating to the able child.
- To meet the needs of advanced development within the mainstream curriculum.
- To provide a range of extension material that will meet the demand for enrichment within the curriculum.
- To incorporate intellectual challenge through the quality rather than the quantity of work.
- To provide self-initiated and self-directed learning that will encourage the able child to develop the knowledge that is worth pursuing.
- To prepare them for an understanding of one's relationships to persons and society.
- To develop a skills-based curriculum that will provide the necessary stimulating work.

The fourth current postholder is a member of the junior department and has, for 18 months, had a monitoring role. We continue to add to our resources on a regular basis but with the advent of the Education Reform Act, and in particular the National Curriculum, we will need to ensure that the differentiated curriculum continues to be addressed. For after all, in the words of Cardinal Newman, 'to live is to change and to be perfect is to have changed often'.

(Johanna Raffan, Holyport CE Primary School)

## Cedars School (urban comprehensive)

*Extending our teaching and our students' learning*

Introduction
Learning is the main function and central activity of the school and each teacher constantly seeks to maximise learning for each student. GCSE,

TVEI and the National Curriculum have all brought with them a reconsideration of the ways we teach and the ways in which our students learn. Moreover, recent involvement with Geoff Grounds, David George and the IAS has made us focus more sharply as a whole school on developing our teaching and learning styles.

Rationale
We believe that our prime task is to create the most appropriate learning environment so that students are able to go as far and as fast as they can. To achieve this, we need to create the widest possible variety of learning opportunities with differentiated activities that recognise different learning rates, styles, interests and abilities.

Policy
Each curricular team and each member of staff is responsible for actively developing varied learning opportunities for our students, for ensuring that students have access to as wide a range of resources as possible, and for seeking ways of increasing the student centred nature of work. However, developments need to be centrally co-ordinated so that we learn from each other, avoid unnecessary duplication of effort and maximise resources, especially the precious resource of staff time.

Intended outcomes
- Staff will provide a greater variety and improved balance of flexible learning opportunities.
- Tasks will be better geared to meeting the needs of individual students and provide greater opportunity for developing higher order skills.
- Students will take greater responsibility for their own learning.
- Student enjoyment of learning and motivation will increase, and we shall be even more successful in translating potential into performance.
- Students, especially the more able, will be given more demanding activities.
- Students will be presented with a wider range of resources.
- There will be a greater opportunity for individual work with students.
- Larger group sizes will be reduced wherever feasible.
- There will be an increase in small group work.
- There will be increased emphasis on study skills and on learning how to learn.
- Resource areas, in particular the library, will undergo major change to facilitate student learning.
- Certain departments will provide specialised opportunities for independent learning.
- There will be greater dialogue within and between departments about teaching and learning.

- There will be greater shadowing of students and observation of colleagues' lessons.
- Increased use will be made of ancillary staff to support teachers.
- We shall work more closely with our middle schools.
- There will be a smoother transition between Year 11 and Year 12 work.

Monitoring

Monitoring will be partly by departmental review and partly through review by the Curriculum Group. It will focus on discussion as to developments, using the department sheets in section 5 as a basis for both review and forward planning. A yearly summary of progress will be produced.

Further points

(1) It is recognised that much staff development will occur through developing teaching and learning styles.

(2) The school is now a member of the National Association for Curriculum Enrichment and copies of its publications (School Policy on Able Children, Identification, Writing Curriculum Enrichment Materials, Resource Lists for Mathematics, Science and Technology) are available in the library.


**Faringdon School**

Faringdon School, a comprehensive in a market town, developed its interest through the enthusiasm of its deputy head. The resulting approach was different, but demonstrates well the flexibility of enrichment and extension as a method of provision.

(1) It started by accident. Some INSET days are tedious, other change your life. Listening to David George at Nene College, Northampton, opened up a whole new way of thought to me and made me realise how inadequate it was simply to provide a 'top set' as a school response to the more able child.

(2) I joined the school to the National Association for Curriculum Enrichment, of which David George is the President, read their leaflets and attended their annual conference. Dr George came very willingly to Faringdon to speak to the staff to raise awareness and challenge them.

(3) One or two little things started to happen. I ran a lunchtime Spanish group in two half hours a week for about ten months, in an attempt to catch the last of the O levels. It was a mixed group of able third years and interested lower six-formers. I did not exclude anyone from opting in from my top set. Consequently some did (whom I would not have advised), some did not (who could have coped). In the event, the

grades were A, B, $2 \times C$, $2 \times D$ and $3 \times U$. Inconclusive – but a start and some highly motivated children, one of whom has gone on to gain an A in GCSE Latin.

(4) While our pupils are required to find their own work experience at the end of their fourth year, the head of science has been able to make the most of some superb placements locally in scientific and electronic establishments. This has led to the pupils doing extended work experience in these places and being given specific projects to do by the companies. In some cases, the pupil has designed or created something which has been adopted by the company. In one case, having not followed the course at school, a boy entered for A level computer studies at the last minute (in the fifth form) and got a grade C, as well as nine GCSE passes.

(5) An electronics club started at lunchtime. A parent provides regular and significant input to this. The attendance has revealed certain youngsters whom one could describe as 'talented' rather than 'more able'. We have been surprised at the skill shown by some of our pupils in this area which has not come out in other sections of the curriculum.

(6) A pupil has come to light in our first year who is years ahead in French – he is functioning at good fourth-year standard. We have, therefore, taken the plunge and decided to teach him individually using a variety of materials: books, videos, cassettes and computer programmes. A pupil of this type raises all sorts of curriculum questions about the phrase in everybody's brochure which says 'we value the education of each child equally'.

(7) In response to my circular colleagues have approached me offering to run Latin as an interest/exam course and there is talk of reintroducing a competitive chess club.

(8) A colleague is working with a pupil deemed to be 'on strike' by his primary school who, according to tests, appears to have a very high IQ. At the moment, on an individual basis, computer programmes – both doing and writing – are being put in his way with good results.

(9) Now that I have passed on the overall responsibility for special needs in the school to a fellow deputy head, I am able to devote more time to finding a school attitude to this phenomenon. I have now circulated the staff with some ideas for purchasing some self-support and self-marking materials, for contacting parents and for making more use of lunchtimes and extension materials. We have in existence a cross-curriculum group, the Special Needs Curriculum Group, where this can be debated.

Thus we have arrived at take-off point!

Richard Arrowsmith

## Programme evaluation

An evaluation of the gifted and talented programmes should be based on the areas and objectives of the programme and be diagnostic. Various points of view should be sought and involve the children, parents, teachers and management of the school. The evaluation scheme should be on-going and thereby allow quick reaction to faults and strengths. This will enable planning, development and accountability from a natural sequence of educational objectives. It must be recognised that the evaluation of these programmes requires the awareness of the problems associated with assessing higher level objectives, the unsuitability of conventionally standardised tests and the practical demand on time, money and trained personnel. The evaluation could take the form of pre and post tests, teacher, parent and children questionnaires – above all, ask the children, who have so much to contribute (Endean and George, 1982).

## Workshop tasks

Identify a group leader and secretary. Prepare an OHP and report back to all course members.

(1) Discuss strategies for identifying the more able children in your school.

(2) What are the principal issues to be addressed in establishing provision for the special needs of more able students in the secondary comprehensive/primary school?

(3) How can these issues be tackled successfully?

(4) What are the most effective ways of supporting colleagues in providing enrichment and challenge in the classroom?

(5) Plan a strategy of identification of underachievement and examine causes of failure to achieve in these individuals.

(6) How is it possible to stimulate bored, underachieving teenagers? How can subjects such as science, history, geography and English be made to come alive and challenge bright underachievers?

(7) Discuss a future school policy for the children in your school and suggest five areas for implementation.

(8) How do you identify a child who is an early second language learner?

(9) In the light of your school's experience of gifted and able children, share thoughts on the challenges they present to you, your school and (where you have the knowledge) their parents. Your recent observation of a gifted/able child in your own school may be relevant to the discussion.

## Epilogue

Sometimes I look about me with a feeling of complete dismay.
In the confusion that afflicts the world today, I see a
Disrespect for the very values of life.
Beauty is all about us, but how many are blind to it!
They look at the wonder of this earth – and seem to see nothing.
Each second we live in a new and unique moment of the universe,
A moment that never was before and will never be again.
And what do we teach our children in school?
We teach them that two and two make four, and that Paris is
the capital of France.
When will we also teach them what they are?

We should say to each of them: do you know what you are?
You are a marvel. You are unique.
In all of the world there is no other child exactly like you.
In the millions of years that have passed, there has never
been another child like you.
And look at your body – what a wonder it is!
Your legs, your arms, your cunning fingers, the way you move!
You may become a Shakespeare, a Michelangelo, a Beethoven.
You have the capacity for anything.
Yes, you are a marvel. And when you grow up,
Can you then harm another who is, like you, a marvel?
You must cherish one another.
You must work – we must all work – to make this world worthy
Of its children.

(Pablo Casals)

# An Introduction to the National Curriculum

The 1988 Education Reform Act has brought about a major change to the education system in England and Wales. To quote the Act:

> The curriculum for every maintained school shall comprise a basic curriculum ... [which] shall comprise the core and other foundation subjects and specify in relation to each of them:
>
> (a) the knowledge, skills and understanding which pupils of different abilities and maturities are expected to have at the end of each key stage;
>
> (b) the matters, skills and processes which are required to be taught to pupils of different abilities and maturities during each key stage;
>
> (c) the arrangements for assessing pupils at or near the end of each key stage for the purpose of ascertaining what they have achieved in relation to the attainment targets for that stage.

The basic curriculum consists of ten subjects; the core subjects of English Maths and Science, and the foundation subjects of Technology, History Geography, Music, Art, PE and a Modern Foreign Language.

The careful exploration of programmes of study both of the core and foundation subjects and the setting of attainment targets coupled with the non-statutory guidance from the National Curriculum Council, have made available to parents and teachers the clearest guidelines on progression ever available.

In the past, dissatisfied parents of the most able might go to their children's schools to protest that their children were not being 'stretched' and were bored, or might even have presented confirmation of the child's high IQ in asking for more demanding work. Now they will be able to claim, with assurance, that their children can attain level x, y or z. The teaching profession will need to consider how to respond to such legitimate claims and to devise ways and means of providing for children well in advance of average peers of the same age. There is no suggestion in the

tional Curriculum that key stage targets should be age-locked and a
able view of the ages at which able children can take public examinations
)ecoming more flexible.

The National Curriculum is built around a system of assessment. There is
)asic framework which consists of ten assessment levels. This has been set
it as follows: At age 7 most pupils would achieve levels 1, 2 or 3; at age 11
vels 3-5; at age 14 levels 4-7 and at age 16 levels 7-10. Within these levels
ach subject is divided up into 'attainment targets'. These are basically the
kills and knowledge the child needs in one aspect of the subject. These
ttainment targets are further broken down into 'levels of attainment'.
hese set out the criteria which must be met for a child to attain a particular
:vel.

The emphasis of National Curriculum is on progressive learning and
ttainment. The child works through the subjects at his/her own pace, and
he teacher can see what the child is good at, and not so good at.

There are also 'key stages' of assessment at ages 7, 11, 14 and 16 and
)upils in every school in the country will be assessed by 'Standard
Assessment Tasks'. These tasks will set targets which establish what
hildren will be expected to know at these ages – and because the SATs will
e national tests, the progress of each child can be measured against
ational standards. The SATs will not be 'tests'; they are ways of assessing
ie stage a child has reached in his/her learning.

It is quite clear that the implementation of the National Curriculum could
ave enormous significance for able and talented children in our schools.
here is still considerable anxiety amongst teachers that it will constrain
nem to concentrate solely on the core and foundation subjects of the
National Curriculum and mitigate against an integral approach to learning.
For our more able children, who frequently interest themselves in a wide
range of subjects in both breadth and depth, it is important that teachers
exercise the flexibility which the Act retains for them in matters of teaching
methods, timetabling and time allocation.

To summarise, the National Curriculum requires by law, a basic
curriculum of core and foundation subjects to be taught. Pupils'
performance in these subjects will be continually assessed, and specific
criteria will be laid down to ascertain what level of skill and knowledge
should be reached at each of ten stages. These skills and knowledge will be
nationally assessed in four key stages and the results of key stages 2, 3 and 4
will be published.

The Act assumes that most children will reach ATs 6 or 7, but also that
some will reach 9 or 10. However, there is little cognisance of the wider
abilities found in any one class of children, nor of their different needs, and
the contents are the same for all and the curriculum content is the same for
all.

# Bibliography

Barbe, W. B. and Renzulli, J. S. (eds) (1975) *Psychology and Education of the Gifted*. John Wiley, New York.

Betts, G. (1985) *Autonomous Learner Model: For the Gifted and Talented*. Grealey, CO; Autonomous Learning Publications and Specialists.

Binet, A. and Simon, T. (1905) 'Methods nouvelles pour le diagnostic du niveau intelletual des anormaux'. *L'Annee Psychologique*, 11, 191–244.

Birch, J., Tisdall, W., Barney, D. and Marks, C. (1965) *A Field Demonstration of the Effectiveness and Feasibility of the Early Admission to School*. University of Pittsburg.

Blakeslee, T. R. (1980) *The Right Brain*. MacMillan Press Limited.

Bloom, B. S. (1985) *Developing Talent in Young People*. Ballantine Books, New York.

Branch, M. and Cash, A. (1966) *Gifted Children: Recognising and Developing Exceptional Ability*. Souvenir Press.

Brierley, J. K. (1973) *The Thinking Machine*. Heinemann.

Brierley, J. K. (1978) *Growing and Learning*. Ward Lock.

Brody, L. and Benbow, C. P. (1987) 'Acceleration Strategies: How Effective Are They?' *Gifted Children Quarterly*, 31, 105–10.

Burt, C. (1975) *The Gifted Child*. Hodder & Stoughton.

Butler-Por, N. (1987) *Gifted Underachievers*. John Wiley.

Clark, B. (1988) *Growing Up Gifted*. Merrill, Columbus, Ohio.

Clarke, G. (1988) *Identification of Gifted Pupils*. Longman, London.

Coleman, L. (1985) *Schooling the Gifted*. Addison-Wesley, Reading, MA.

Csikszenmihalyi, M. and Robinson, R. E. (1986) 'Culture, Time and the Development of Talent'. In R. J. Sternberg and J. E. Davidson.

Davis, G. A. and Rimm, S. B. (1989) *Education of the Gifted and Talented*. Prentice Hall.

de Bono, E. (1973) *CORT Thinking*. Pergamon, New York.

Denton, C. and Postlethwaite, K. (1985) *Able Children*. NFER-Nelson.

DES (1977) 'Gifted Children in Middle and Comprehensive Schools'. HMI Series, *Matters for Discussion*, 4. HMSO.

DES (1978) 'The Development of Sporting Talent in Children of School Age'. Circular 16/78 (Joint Circular).

DES (1985) *Better Schools*. HMSO.

DES (1985) 'The Curriculum 5-16'. An HMI Series. HMSO. p. 28.

Endean, L. and George, D. R. (1982) 'Observing Thirty Able Young Scientists'. *School Science Review*.

Eyre, D. and Marjoram, T. (1990) *Enriching and Extending the National Curriculum*. Kogan Page, London.

Feldhusen, J. F. (ed) (1985) *Towards Excellence in Gifted Education*. Love Publishing.

Feldhusen, J. F. and Kolloff, P. B. (1981) 'A Three-Stage Model for Gifted Children'. In Classen *et al. Programming for the Gifted and Talented and Creative*. University of Wisconsin.

Feldhusen, J. F. and Treffinger, D. J. (1985) *Creative Thinking and Problem Solving in Gifted Education*. Dubuque: Kendall/Hunt.

Feldman, D. H. (1982) *Developmental Approaches to Giftedness*. Jossey-Bass.

Flack, G. (1990) *Creativity*. G.T. News, University of Colorado.

Freeman, J. (1979) *Gifted Children: Their Identification and Development in a Social Context*. International Medical Press, Lancaster.

Freeman, J. (1981) *Clever Children: A Parents' Guide*. Hamlyn, London.

Freeman, J. (ed) (1985) *The Psychology of Gifted Children*. John Wiley.

Freeman, J. (1991) *Gifted Children Growing Up*. Cassell, London.

Gagne, F. (1985) 'Giftedness and Talent: Re-examining a Re-examination of the Definitions'. *Gifted Children Quarterly*, 29, 103–12.

Gallagher, J. J. (1985) *Teaching the Gifted Child*. Allyn & Bacon, New York.

Gardner, J. W. (1961) *How Can We Be Excellent and Equal Too?* Harper & Row, New York.

Gear, G. (1978) 'Effects of Training on Teachers' Accuracy in the Identification of Gifted Children'. *Gifted Children Quarterly*, 21, p. 90.

George, D. R. (1990) 'The Challenge of the Able Child'. *Cantab. J. Ed.*, Vol. 20, No. 2.

George, W. C. (ed)(1979) *Educating the Gifted: Acceleration and Enrichment*. Johns Hopkins University Press.

Getzels, J. and Jackson, P. (1962) *Creativity and Intelligence*. John Wiley, New York.

Gold, M. (1979) 'Acceleration: Simplistic Gimmickry'. In George (ed) (1979).

Guilford, J. P. (1967) *The Nature of Human Intelligence*. McGraw-Hill, New York.

Guilford, J. P. (1977) *War Beyond the IQ*. Creative Education Foundation, Buffalo, NY.

Harvey, S. and Steeley, J. (1984) 'An Investigation into Relationships Among Intelligence, Creative Abilities, Extra-Curricular Activities, Achievement and Giftedness in a Delinquent Population'. *Gifted Children Quarterly*, 28, 73–9.

Heller, K. A. and Feldhusen, J. F. (ed) (1988) *Identifying and Nurturing the Gifted: An International Perspective*. Hans Huber, Toronto.

Herrmann, N. (1987) *The Application of Brain Dominance Technology to the Training Profession*. 7th World Conference, Salt Lake City.

Hitchfield, E. M. (1973) *In Search of Promise*. Longman, London.

HMSO (1977) *Gifted Children in Middle and Comprehensive Secondary Schools*. HMSO, London.

HMSO (1985) *Good Teachers*. HMSO.

HMSO (1985) *Ten Good Schools*. HMSO.

HMSO (1988) *Secondary Schools – An Approach*. HMSO.

Howe, J. A. (1990) *Sense and Nonsense About Hothouse Children*. British Psychological Society, Leicester.

Howley, A., Howley, C. and Pendarvis, E. (1986) *Teaching Gifted Children: Principles and Strategies*. Little, Brown & Co., Boston.

Jellen, H. G. and Urban, K. K. (1989) 'Assessing Creative Potential World-wide'. *Gifted Education Int.*, 6, 78–86.

Jones, C. A. (1986) *Developing Physical Skills to Full Potential*. National Association for Curriculum Enrichment Publications.

Kamin, L. G. (1974) *The Science and Politics of IQ*. Penguin.

Kerry, T. (1983) *Finding and Helping the Able Child*. Croom Helm.

Kirschenbaum, R. (1987) 'Enrichment Programming for Gifted and Talented High School Students'. *Roeper Review*, 10, 117-18.

Kitano, M. and Kirby, D. (1986) *Gifted Education: A Comprehensive View*. Little Brown, Boston.

Klein, R. (1982) 'An Inquiry Into Factors Related to Creativity'. *Elementary School Journal*, 82, 256-66.

Leyden, S. (1985) *Helping Children of Exceptional Ability*. Croom Helm.

Lock, R. and Jay, G. (1987) 'Self-Concept in Gifted Children: Differential Input in Boys and Girls'. *Gifted Children Quarterly*, 31, 9-14.

Magoon, R. A. (1981) 'A Proposed Model for Leadership Development'. *Roeper Review*, 3, 7-9.

Maker, C. J. (1982) *Curriculum Development for the Gifted*. Aspen. Systems Corporation.

Maker, C. J. (1982) *Teaching Models in Education of the Gifted*. Aspen Systems Corporation.

Maltby, F. (1984) *Gifted Children and Teachers in Primary Schools*. Falmer Press.

Marland, S. (1972) *Education of the Gifted and Talented*. Report to Congress. US Office of Information.

Maslow, A. H. (1954) *Motivation and Personality*. Harper & Row, New York.

Mason, P. (1987) *The Social, Educational and Emotional Needs of Gifted Children*. Cicely Northcote Trust.

McAlpine, D. S. (1988) *Creativity: Teaching Processes and Teaching Implications*. NACE Publications.

Meeker, M. N. and Meeker, R. (1986) 'The SOI System for Gifted Education'. In J. S. Renzulli (ed) *Systems and Models for Developing Programmes for the Gifted and Talented*. Creative Learning Press, Mansfield Centre.

NAGC (1989) *Help With Bright Children*.

NAGC (1990) *Survey of Provision for Able and Talented Children*.

NAGC (1990) *According to their Needs*.

NCC (1989) *A Curriculum for All - Curriculum Guidance 2*.

NCC (1990) *The Whole Curriculum - Curriculum Guidance 3*.

NCC (1990) *Core Skills*.

National Society for the Study of Education (1979) *The Gifted and the Talented: Their Education and Development*. NSSE.

Newland, T. E. (1976) *The Gifted in Socioeducational Perspective*. Prentice Hall, New York.

Novak, D. and Goodwin, B. (1984) *Learning How to Learn*. CUP.

Ogilvie, E. (1973) *Gifted Children in Primary Schools*. Macmillan, London.

Painter, F. (1980) *Meeting the Needs of the Gifted in Schools*. Pullen Pubs.

Painter, F. (1984) *Living with a Gifted Child*. Souvenir.

Parry, S. J. (1977) 'The Concept of Excellence in Sport'. In NATFE Conference Report.

Pegnato, C. and Birch, J. (1959) 'Locating Gifted Children in Junior High Schools'. *Exceptional Children*, 25, 300-4.

Plowman, P. D. (1981) 'Training Extraordinary Leaders'. *Roeper Review* 3(3), 13-16.

Postlethwaite, K. (1988) *Organising the School's Response*. Macmillan Education.

Povey, R. (ed) (1980) *Educating the Gifted Child*. Harper & Row, London.

Proctor, T. B., Black, K. N. and Feldhusen, J. F. (1986) 'Early Admission of Selected Children to Elementary School: A Review of the Research Literature'. *Journal of Education Research*, 80(2).

Renzulli, J. S. (1977) *The Enrichment Triad Model: A Guide for Developing Defensible Programs for the Gifted and Talented*. Creative Learning Press.

Renzulli, J. S. (1988) *The Multiple Menu Model for Developing Differentiated Curriculum for the Gifted and Talented*. Univ. of Connecticut.

Renzulli, J. S., Reis, S. M. and Smith, L. H. (1981) *The Revolving Door Identification Model*. Creative Learning Press.

Renzulli, J. S., Smith, L., White, A., Callahan, C. and Hartman, R. (1977) *Scale for Rating the Behavioural Characteristics of Superior Students*. Creative Learning Press.

Reynolds, M. C., Birch, J. W. and Tuseth, A. A. (1976) 'Research on Early Admission'. In W. Dennis and M. Dennis (eds) *The Intellectually Gifted*. Grune & Stratton, New York.

Rimm, S. B. (1989) *Underachievement Syndrome: Causes and Cures*. Apple Pub. Co., Waterdown, WI.

Rimm, S. B. (1990) *How to Parent a Child So Children Will Learn*. Apple Pub.

Rimm, S. B. (1990) 'Underachievement Syndrome: Causes, Preventions and Cures. *Exceptionality Ed.*, Canada, Vol. 1, No. 1.

Rogers, C. R. (1962) 'Towards a Theory of Creativity'. In S. J. Parnes and H. F. Harding (eds) *A Source Book for Creative Thinking*. Scribers, New York.

Shore, B. M. (1981) *Face to Face with Giftedness*. 1st Yearbook of 1981 World Conference, World Council for Gifted Children.

Shore, B. M. (1991) 'Building a Professional Knowledge Base'. *Exceptionality Ed.* Canada, Vol. 1, No. 1.

Silverman, L. K. (1986) The IQ Controversy. *Roeper Review*, Vol. 8, No. 3.

Sports Council (1984) Annual Report, 1983/84, p. 6.

Stanley, J. C., Keating, D. and Fox, L. (ed) (1974) *Mathematical Talent: Discovery, Description and Development*. Johns Hopkins University Press.

Sternberg, R. and Davidson, J. E. (1986) Conceptions of Giftedness. CUP.

Straker, A. (1983) *Mathematics for Gifted Pupils*. Longman.

Tannenboum, A. J. (1983) *Gifted Children*. Macmillan.

Taylor, C. W. (1978) 'How Many Types of Giftedness Can Your Programme Tolerate?'. *Journal of Creative Behaviour*, 12, 39–51.

Taylor, C. W. (ed) (1990) *Expanding Awareness of Creative Potentials Worldwide*. Seventh World Conference on Gifted and Talented Children. Trillium Press, New York.

Taylor, R. L. and Sternberg, L. (1989) *Exceptional Children*. Springer-Verlag.

Teare, J. B. (1988) *A School Policy on Provision for Able Pupils*. NACE.

Teare, J. B. (1988) *Able Pupils: Practical Identification Strategies*. NACE.

Tempest, N. R. (1974) *Teaching Clever Children 7–11*. Routledge & Kegan Paul.

Terman, L. M. (1981) 'The Discovery and Encouragement of Exceptional Talent'. In W. B. Barbe and J. S. Renzulli (1975/3rd Edn).

Terman, L. M. and Oden, M. H. (1947, 1959) *Genetic Study of Genius: The Gifted Child Grows Up*. Stanford University Press, Stanford, CA.

Tilsley, P. (1979) 'Gifted Children and Their Education'. *Journal of App. Ed. St.*, 8, 1.

Torrance, E. P. (1977) *Discovering and Nurturance of Giftedness in the Culturally Different*. Council for Exceptional Children, Reston, VA.

Torrance, E. P. (1980) 'Assessing the Further Reaches of Creative Potential'. *Journal of Creative Behaviour*, 14, 1–19.

Treffinger, D. J. (1975) 'Teaching for Self-directed Learning: A Priority for the Gifted and Talented'. *Gifted Children Quarterly*, 19, 46–59.

Treffinger, D. J. and Renzulli, J. S. (1986) 'Giftedness as Potential for Creative Productivity Transcending IQ Scores'. *Roeper Review*, 8(3), 150–4.

University of Leicester (1979) *The Bright Child in the Comprehensive School Teacher Education Project*.

148

Urban, K. K. (1988) *Recent Trends in Creativity*. Paper given at ECHA Conference, Zurich.

Vaughan, M. M. (1977) 'Musical Creativity: Its Cultivation and Measurement'. *Bull. Co. Res. Mus. Ed.*, 50 (72-7).

Vernon, P. E. (1977) *The Psychology and Education of Gifted Children*. Methuen, London.

Wallace, A. (1986) *The Prodigy*. Macmillan.

Wallace, B. (1983) *Teaching the Very Able Child*. Ward Lock Educational.

Warnock Report (1978) *GB DES Committee of Enquiry into the Education of Handicapped Children and Young People*. HMSO.

White, B. L., Kaban, B. T. and Attanucci, J. (1979) *The Origins of Human Competence: The Final Report of the Harvard Pre-school Project*. Lexington Books, Massachusetts.

Williams, F. E. (1970) *Classroom Ideas for Encouraging Thinking and Teaching*. DOK Publishers, Buffalo, New York.

Willings, D. (1980) *The Creatively Gifted: Recognising and Developing the Creative Personality*. Woodhead Faulkner, Cambridge.

Wittgenstein, L. (1958) *Philosophical Investigations*. Basil Blackwell, Oxford.

# Index